W9-DES-241

LET'S-TALK-ABOUT-IT STORIES FOR KIDS

You're Worth More Than You Think!

LOIS WALFRID JOHNSON

Illustrations by Virginia Peck

NAVPRESS

A MINISTRY OF THE NAVIGATORS
P.O. BOX 6000, COLORADO SPRINGS, COLORADO 80934

The Navigators is an international Christian organization. Jesus Christ gave His followers the Great Commission to go and make disciples (Matthew 28:19). The aim of The Navigators is to help fulfill that commission by multiplying laborers for Christ in every nation.

NavPress is the publishing ministry of The Navigators. NavPress publications are tools to help Christians grow. Although publications alone cannot make disciples or change lives, they can help believers learn biblical discipleship, and apply what they learn to their lives and ministries.

CONTENTS

To Kids Who Read This Book —— 11

The Long Swim —— 15

First Day for Erin —— 23

March Wind —— 29

A Present for Chris —— 37

You're My Friend —— 45

Angelo Carries the Pigskin —— 51

Christmas Love —— 57

After the Play —— 63

Nikki Looks in the Mirror —— 69

Mess in the Garage —— 75

Cathy's Song —— 83

I Can't Help Wondering —— 89

What Should I Do? —— 95

Better Than an "A" —— 101

Something to Offer —— 107

Corey Goes to Camp —— 113

Grandma's Story —— 119

Tell Me More —— 127

Bugs Bunny Klumpers —— 133

From the Pitcher's Mound —— 139

How's My Mom? —— 147

I'm Different —— 153

More Than Hot Lunch —— 159

He's My Brother —— 165

A Phone of My Own —— 173

For In-Spite-of-It Kids —— 179

To Ken and Claire Wesloh,
who are worth more than they know

AUTHOR

When Lois Walfrid Johnson was nine years old she wondered, "What do I want to be when I grow up?" She sensed God's call to be a writer. If she could possibly write a book, she wanted to tell others what she believed about Jesus Christ.

That desire stayed with her through high school, college, and the early years of her marriage to Roy Johnson, an elementary school teacher. When the youngest of their three children entered first grade, Lois became a full-time free-lance writer. Her articles, poetry, and books have been published in English-speaking countries throughout the world and translated into nine languages.

Lois Johnson is the author of thirteen books,

including *Secrets of the Best Choice, Thanks for Being My Friend,* and *You Are Wonderfully Made!* in the *LET'S-TALK-ABOUT-IT* series. She has also written *Just a Minute, Lord* and *You're My Best Friend, Lord* for pre-teens; *Come as You Are* for young teens; *Gift in My Arms, Either Way,* and *Falling Apart or Coming Together* for adults. Lois leads seminars and retreats and speaks at churches and conferences throughout the United States.

ACKNOWLEDGMENTS

My gratitude to the Lord Jesus Christ and these other builders of my self-esteem: Cliff Bjork and Kevin Johnson for helping me become computer-wise; Traci Mullins, Jerry Foley, Charette Kvernstoen, Pat Rosenberg, Penny Stokes, and Terry White for help with the manuscript; my husband, Roy, for his insight, love, and daily encouragement.

TO KIDS WHO READ THIS BOOK

Have you ever faced something you thought you couldn't do? Did it seem you were fighting a lion or bear? Did you wonder if you could win?

Maybe you told yourself, "I'm not good enough. I can't do it." If you did, you have lots of company. It's easy to feel like that.

But there's another way, one that a young boy named David knew.

David had hard things to face. Everything didn't go the way he wanted. To save his father's sheep he had to kill lions and bears. Even worse, God sent him to fight a giant!

Goliath was a nine-foot-tall soldier in the Philistine army. Morning and evening for forty days he shouted threats to the army of Israel, God's chosen nation. "Choose one of your men to fight me! If he kills me, we'll be your slaves. If I kill him, you'll be *our* slaves!"

Goliath frightened Saul, the king of Israel, and his soldiers. As they listened to his threats, they became afraid to fight back. But when David heard Goliath's words, he asked, "Who is this Philistine that threatens the army of the living God?"

Overhearing his question, his older brother asked him, "Who do you think *you* are?"

Then King Saul said to David, "You're only a boy. Goliath has been a soldier all his life!"

Yet David took his slingshot, collected five stones from the creek, and started toward the giant.

Goliath saw he was only a boy. He poked fun at David, shouting, "Come here! I'll give your body to the birds and animals to eat!"

"You come against me with a sword and a spear," David called back. "But I come against you in the name of the Lord Almighty, the God of the armies of Israel. It's not by sword or spear that the Lord saves, for the battle is the Lord's."

Goliath moved closer, and David ran forward to meet him. Taking a stone, he hurled it from his sling and struck Goliath on the forehead.

The giant fell face down on the ground. Then

David took Goliath's own sword and killed him.

When you think about David, you may tell yourself, "I couldn't do what he did."

That's right, you couldn't. But David had a secret source of power. He didn't trust in what *he* could do. David knew God. He knew what God could do for him. David had a godly self-esteem.

You might wonder, "What *is* self-esteem?"

It's not the feeling that you're better than everyone else. Nor is it the belief that your way is always best. Self-esteem is not even thinking that you deserve the best, or at least whatever you want. Self-esteem means having a healthy respect for yourself based on what God thinks about you.

If you don't like yourself, it's hard to love and help others. You feel as weak as a newborn puppy needing milk to stay alive. But when you have godly self-esteem, you know God. You know you belong to Him. You know you are valuable just the way you are. You know you are loved. You believe you have something to offer others. Like David, you belong to a club for in-spite-of-it kids.

The true-to-life stories in this book tell about boys and girls who face problems like yours, or like those of your friends. They need to make choices—whether to lose their battles or accept God's help and win. They need to decide whether they'll become in-spite-of-it kids.

If you're such a kid, you know that some things in your life are not the way you want. Sometimes you feel like you're losing. Yet you believe God is in control. You believe God can help you with whatever you face.

When you talk about the questions at the end of each story, you'll see new ways of making choices. You'll think about how to deal with things that bother you.

Then turn the book upside down. Repeat the Bible verse to yourself until you receive the help it gives. Say the prayer, or one of your own words. Learn to believe in a big God.

God the Father created you. His Son, Jesus, loves you so much that He died for you. The Holy Spirit wants to encourage you, to give you the power and help you need. To Them you are worth more than you can even guess.

YOU'RE WORTH MORE THAN YOU THINK!

THE LONG SWIM

Mickey peered out the window as his dad backed into the camping spot. Around the car, pine trees formed a windbreak for the tent they would pitch. Far below, the Pacific Ocean beat against a sandy beach.

"Everybody out," said Dad. "As soon as we're set up, we can swim."

Mickey followed his older brother Troy from the car and helped Mom take out the food. While she spread a cloth on the picnic table, Mickey set a cake on the bench. Dad and Troy lifted the tent from the trunk.

As soon as Troy checked over the campsite, he started telling Mickey what to do. "Spread out the ground tarp," he said. "Get the hammer." Then, "Hold the stake on that side, while I pound one in over here."

At first Mickey didn't mind. Troy always got things done. "I wish I could be like him," thought Mickey, as he'd often wished before. Besides, the quicker the tent went up, the longer they'd have to swim.

Yet as soon as that was finished, Troy gave more orders. "I saw the pump that way." Tossing Mickey two large jugs, he pointed toward a path.

Mickey set out quickly, still looking forward to being in the ocean. He liked to swim, and it was the one thing he could do better than Troy. Mickey practiced more and learned new strokes by watching older kids.

Even so, as he started back with the water, his steps slowed. "Why does Troy always have to be the boss?" he asked himself.

The trail led uphill, and the jugs got heavier with each step. Mickey grew hot and sweaty as the jugs bumped against his knees. "What a drag," he thought. "Why couldn't Troy do this?"

Nearing the campsite, he heard Dad call out to Troy. "Good job, Son. We're setting up in less time every day."

Mickey knew Dad was right. Troy had done a good job. But a little twinge of something bothered Mickey. Somehow he felt worthless—as though he could never keep up.

As he came into the clearing, Mickey tried to carry the jugs the way Troy usually did—as though it was the easiest thing in the world. Yet as he leaned forward to put them on the picnic table, he stumbled. The weight of the jugs threw him off balance. As one knee landed on the bench, Mickey felt the squish of something soft.

"Oh, no, my cake!" wailed Mom.

Looking down, Mickey saw his knee planted squarely in the cakepan. Around its tinfoil covering, chocolate cake and white frosting oozed out on the bench.

Dad and Troy laughed. Mickey tried to laugh too, but didn't quite make it. The hot flush of embarrassment reached his face as Mom wiped cake off his jeans. He felt like a little kid.

"Troy would never do such a stupid thing," Mickey thought, wishing he could crawl inside a hollow stump.

But soon everyone changed clothes and went down to the beach. As far as Mickey could see, there was only sand and water and the waves lapping against the shore. Off to the west the sun edged earthward, casting a golden path on the water.

Mom and Dad stretched out on large towels, and Mickey followed Troy into the surf. Looking at his brother's height, Mickey felt puny. But the cold water felt good. Again and again he waded in, turned, dropped on his stomach, and rode the waves to shore.

While they swam, the sun dropped lower. As Mickey waded back into deeper water, he looked out to the horizon. Squinting, he felt blinded by the light. It was hard to see Troy, but he was out there again, ahead of him.

Knowing Mom and Dad wanted them to stay together, Mickey headed into the waves, striking out toward the sun. But Troy kept moving farther away. Mickey felt uneasy, knowing Troy shouldn't go out that far, wondering if Mom and Dad could see him.

Half walking, half swimming, Mickey hurried to catch up. Once he called out, "Hey, Troy!" But Troy didn't turn, and Mickey guessed that the noise of the surf drowned out his voice.

Now Mickey felt an urgency to catch up to his brother. Were the waves growing larger, or did it just seem that way? He'd almost reached Troy when he heard his brother cry out.

Panic filled Troy's voice. Diving into the waves, Mickey swam as fast as he could toward his brother. Coming to the surface, he looked around and at the same time stretched one leg down. He couldn't touch bottom. Mickey knew Troy must have felt the ground fall away and panicked. Or had a strong current pulled him off balance?

Mickey swam a few more feet and grabbed Troy's arm, ready to pull him toward shore. But Troy lashed

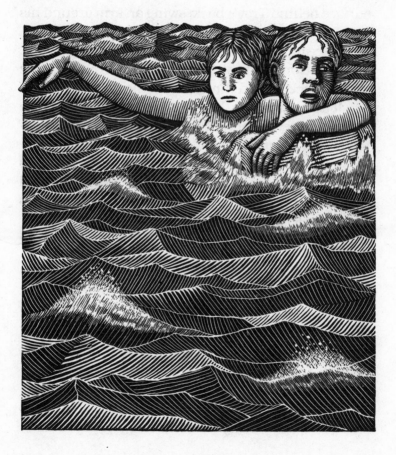

out, swinging wildly. Grabbing Mickey around the neck, he clung to him.

Mickey gasped for air. Almost out of breath, he plunged under the water, dragging Troy with him. Troy's grip loosened. Somehow Mickey managed to surface behind Troy's back, swing an arm around his chest and start swimming.

Once more Troy struggled, but Mickey's grip held. With a strong arm stroke and a powerful kick, he started back toward shore, letting the waves help him.

It seemed forever, but wasn't more than a minute before Mickey's foot reached down and touched bottom. Never before had sand felt so good.

Helping Troy stand up, Mickey watched his brother draw a deep breath. The waves washed around him, and Troy shivered. But Mickey looked in his eyes and knew something had changed.

"I don't have to be like Troy," he thought. "I can just be me."

TO TALK ABOUT

▶ How can family position make someone like Mickey feel he isn't worth as much as an older brother or sister?

▶ What difference will it make to Mickey to feel he doesn't have to be just like Troy?

▶ Do you think Mickey's parents love one boy more

than the other? Or do they love each boy for his own special qualities? Why do you think so?

▶Sometimes it's good to want to be like someone else. It encourages us to live up to their strong qualities. Other times it's not good because we don't appreciate the way we are. Which was true in Mickey's case? How do you know?

▶It took something very big before Mickey realized he had something to offer. Most of us are not heroes the way he was. But all of us have good qualities that can help us become in-spite-of-it kids. Those qualities are gifts from God, and it's important to know what they are. What good qualities do you have? (Be honest now! It will encourage your self-esteem.)

▶Does God love all of us equally, no matter who we are? Or does He play favorites? How do you know?

▶If you don't have a mom and dad who let you know that they love you for the special person you are, what thought can comfort you?

The Lord will work out his plans for my life—for your lovingkindness, Lord, continues forever.
(Psalm 138:8, TLB)

Help me, Lord, to stop comparing myself with others. Thank You that I have my own set of strengths and good qualities. Thanks that in Your eyes I am never second best.

FIRST DAY FOR ERIN

Ready to leave the bedroom she knew so well, Erin looked once more at her bulletin board. On it were reminders of special times—a dried flower from a wedding, a ticket stub from the Milwaukee Zoo, a picture of her friends on the last day of school.

Seeing the picture, she felt sad for what was past, and afraid of what was ahead. The school district had shut down the small, old building where Erin knew everyone and everything. Her friend Jill would be in the big, new school, but most of the other kids were going elsewhere.

Though the day was bright with sunshine, Erin's heart felt cold. Climbing aboard the school bus she wondered, "What if I can't remember where my classes are? What if I get lost?"

Sure, there had been visiting day. She and Jill and other new kids went through their schedules. But now the school would be full of kids who knew each other and knew where they were going.

Butterflies fluttered in Erin's stomach. "What if— What if they laugh at me?"

Leaving the bus, Erin pulled open the heavy school door. The sunshine disappeared in the long halls and endless classrooms.

"I can't do it," she thought. The words set up a chant in her brain. "I can't do it." Around and around the words went.

"Hi, Erin," called Jill, coming up from behind. "All set?"

Erin's hug said more than words. Jill would remember where to go. She always found her way around.

Jill chattered as she went. "Good thing we have the same schedules." Soon she took a right, then a left, then started down another long hall. Step by step, Erin followed, confused by all the turns.

"I don't remember going this way," she thought, feeling glad Jill took the lead.

"Here it is," said Jill. "Room 111."

The girls slid into seats across from each other. Soon the teacher asked them to open their math books. Looking at the problems, Erin's brain felt fuzzy.

"They're so hard," she whispered to Jill. "You know how dumb I am in math."

When the bell rang, they started out once more. Again Jill took the lead. Turning one way, then another, she climbed a flight of stairs, then rounded a corner.

"I can't remember this either," Erin thought, not wanting to admit she had no idea where they were. "How does Jill manage to do it?"

"Room 238," said Jill, as though she had discovered the New World. As far as Erin was concerned, she had.

It was English class. "She'll ask us to write about what we did this summer," Erin told Jill.

Sure enough. "Do one page," the teacher said.

"That's easy," Erin said in a low voice. "I did lots of fun things."

But as she bent over her paper, she remembered another class and another time. As though it were yesterday, Erin saw herself in fourth grade, trying to write about her summer. That time she couldn't come up with one sentence. Erin still remembered how she felt when the teacher collected her blank paper.

Now, like a recorder in her head, a tape started to play. "You're going to tell about the time on the beach? That doesn't sound like fun."

Erin wrote one sentence, then sat back to look at it. "What if this sounds dumb?" she asked herself.

Crumpling up her paper, Erin tried again. Before she knew it, the time was up. Her paper was still blank, but Jill had written two pages.

The bell rang, and Erin followed Jill out of class. One part of Erin wanted to be like Jill. The other part started to resent all the things Jill did well.

By this time, Erin's fuzzy head felt like splitting. Together they walked down a flight of stairs, around a corner, then into a long hall.

Suddenly Jill stood still. "Where are we? You'll have to help me on this one, Erin."

"You really don't know?"

Jill shook her head.

"But you've taken us around all day."

"You think so? You didn't notice I was going in circles? Or rather in squares?"

"But I thought you knew where you were going."

Jill shook her head. "I didn't know if I could find the rooms. I just kept trying." She grinned. "I figured if I got lost, I could always ask someone—like right now."

Suddenly Erin's fuzzy brain cleared. "All day long I thought. . . ."

Looking around, Erin recognized a display window. This time she didn't listen to the voice that said she couldn't do it. "Come on," she said, wanting to make a new start.

TO TALK ABOUT

▶Erin and Jill faced the same problems, but Erin was afraid of the "what ifs." How did she use those "what ifs" to knock herself? How did Erin's habit of putting herself down keep her from doing things?

▶Why is it better to try and fail than to never try at all?

▶The way you look at yourself can become a mountain that keeps you from trying. You begin believing the negative things you say about yourself. In what ways do you knock yourself?

▶Are you really a failure in a certain area, or is it something you tell yourself? How do you know?

▶Satan wants you to feel you're no good. It's a trick he uses to keep you from reaching your best for Jesus Christ. Instead of dwelling on negative thoughts, let the Holy Spirit help you. Repeat a Bible verse that encourages you. God's Word has the power to change the way you think. What are some helpful verses?

▶How can memorizing such verses help you become an in-spite-of-it kid?

I can do everything God asks me to with the help of Christ who gives me the strength and power. (Philippians 4:13, TLB)

Forgive me, Jesus, for telling myself I can't do things, even before I try. Help me to stop knocking myself. Help me find my confidence and strength in You. Thanks that You can help me reach my best when I trust You.

MARCH WIND

As he left home, Jon felt the wind catch his jacket. It was a brisk Saturday morning in early March, and all week he had thought about launching his new rocket.

"Will the wind be too strong?" he wondered. Rocket under one arm and backpack over his shoulder, he started across the large, vacant field on the edge of the city. The long grass was brown and dry, the ground hilly and uneven.

Moments later he heard Danny's shout. His friend also carried a backpack. Jon knew there'd be food. It'd be a good day.

For an instant he felt a twinge of uneasiness. Dad didn't like to have him with Danny. Twice Danny had gotten him in trouble. But Jon knew Danny liked rockets as much as he did. If anything happened, he could always put the blame on Danny.

The two boys set to work, deciding where to put the launch pad. Jon wanted to avoid the swamp and the telephone lines at the other end of the field.

Soon they had the pad in place, ready to mount the rocket. Jon ran his hands over the smooth lines. "It's the biggest one I've built," he said proudly. "Bet it will go to the moon."

Carefully he set it on the launch pad. Each time Jon put together a rocket he looked forward to this moment. Yet he also felt the tingle of the unknown. "Will it take off?" he wondered. "Will it go the direction I want?"

He knelt, and Danny helped steady the rocket. Jon pressed the ignition button and both of them stepped back. Whoooosh! Up, up, and away!

Suddenly Jon realized he and Danny were shouting with excitement. Against the blue sky, the rocket turned and leveled out.

In the next moment the wind caught the long slender cone. Jon knew it was edging off course. He started to run, trying to keep the rocket in sight. Faster and faster it went—swinging over—over above the swamp—over. . . .

Just then Jon's foot caught a rock. He landed flat on his face, all the wind knocked out of his lungs. He lay still for a moment, unable to move.

Soon Danny was with him. Slowly, carefully, Jon sat up, still trying to catch his breath. "What happened?" he asked between gasps.

"To the rocket? I'm not sure," said Danny.

"Did you see it head toward the swamp?"

"Yep," Danny nodded, his face gloomy. "It couldn't have gone in a worse place."

When Jon could walk, they headed toward the spot where they'd last seen the rocket. Reaching soft ground, Jon tried to step on the clumps of grass. Instead he slipped into cold water. Danny tried another place and went in up to his knees.

After a long search they had to give up. By then both of them were shivering.

"Let's build a fire," said Danny.

"No way," answered Jon. "We're not supposed to."

"But I've got marshmallows. We could toast them."

It wasn't hard for Jon to remember how toasted marshmallows tasted. He was tempted. So far the day had been a bummer.

Then he remembered Dad's words, "Never, never start a fire in that field. It's a tinderbox."

For a moment Jon thought about what Dad had said. He was right. The field was really dry.

"See that spot over by that rock?" asked Danny. "It's not as windy there. We could sit close to the fire, and warm up."

31

"Nah, Dad said . . ." started Jon.

"Just a minute. I'll get what we need," said Danny.

Moments later, he was back with two sticks for toasting, and some dried-out branches for kindling.

Jon had to admit it would feel good to warm up—and the marshmallows. . . . He helped Danny carry the wood over to the sheltered place between the rocks. "We've got to keep it small," he said, pushing his uneasiness aside. He tried to ignore the nudge of his conscience.

"We will," promised Danny.

"If anything happens, it's your fault," said Jon.

"My fault! Whadda ya mean, my fault?"

"It's your idea, and you know it's wrong!" Jon was shouting now.

"Hey, you're in this too! You can't put the blame on me."

Jon still felt uneasy, but Danny had the bag of marshmallows out. Pulling up clumps of long, dry grass, he laid them in a heap. Then he put the small branches on top and lit the grass. Seconds later flames flared up.

Just then a gust of wind circled the rocks, caught the fire, and pushed the flames toward the long grass nearby. Jon jumped up, his uneasiness changing to alarm.

"Hey, it's all right," said Danny. "Nothing will happen."

But fingers of flame reached out, beginning to crawl. Jon pulled off his jacket and beat it against the earth. He tried hard, but couldn't keep up.

A moment later the wind swung around. One small flame from the other side of the campfire reached out, grabbed more grass, and devoured it.

This time Danny jumped up. Already the fire had moved away, eating whatever it touched. "Run!" he shouted.

Jon still pounded his jacket on the ground, trying to get the fire out. But the wind swung again. The fire started off in a new direction. "It's headed toward the houses! Danny, help me!"

"It's too late! Let's get out of here! Run!"

Grabbing their backpacks, the two boys took off toward the houses. Soon they reached a garage. "Hide!" exclaimed Danny. Finding an unlocked door, they stepped inside. For a moment they stood there, gasping and catching their breath.

"We've gotta tell someone," cried Jon. "We've gotta call the fire department!"

"Not on your life!" said Danny.

"But the people in the houses!" More than Jon's conscience hurt him now. He felt panic, thinking about what could happen.

"No way!" answered Danny. "Let's get out of here. We're too close."

Heading out of the garage, they rounded the

corner and moved off down the street.

Just then a fire engine wailed in the distance. "Someone called in," said Jon, panting as he spoke. "They'll get the fire out."

He felt relieved. It was all he could do to keep up with Danny. "If anyone finds out, I'll put the blame on him," Jon told himself.

Stretching out his legs, Jon ran with a speed he didn't know he had. He clung to one thought. "If I can get inside my house, everything will be okay."

But somehow he didn't feel good about himself.

TO TALK ABOUT

▶ Do you agree with Jon, that everything will be okay? What do you think will happen?

▶ Whose fault was it that the fire started?

▶ Sometimes it *seems* like a good idea to blame someone else to keep out of trouble. Yet blaming others can hurt us. How could it hurt Jon if he puts the blame on Danny and gets away with it? How will he feel about himself?

▶ God created us with a conscience to help us recognize the difference between right and wrong. If we say no to our conscience about the wrong things we do, we hide sin in our heart. What will happen to Jon if he keeps saying no to his conscience? How will it affect any relationship he might have with God?

▶We're not free to like ourselves unless things are right between us and God. What might happen to Danny and Jon if no one finds out they started the fire? How would it help them to be found out?
▶What choice do you feel Jon and Danny should make? Why?

I have hidden your word in my heart that I might not sin against you. (Psalm 119:11)

Forgive me, Jesus, for the wrong things I've done— especially the things I seem to have gotten away with. If I need to own up to something, help me to set things right. Help me to stop blaming others. Hide Your Word in my heart so I won't sin against You.

A PRESENT FOR CHRIS

Chris was in his room when the doorbell rang. The sudden jolt to his insides warned him. All through supper he had felt terrible about what he did. Had someone found out?

Quietly he opened his door a crack and listened. It was Mr. Roberts. Chris's misery grew.

"Chrrriiss!" The sound of Dad's voice came up the stairway.

"Maybe I can pretend I'm not here," Chris thought, his guilty feelings exploding like a firecracker. Yet he knew Dad would find him another time.

Again Dad called, and step-by-slow-step Chris went downstairs. He dreaded the look he'd find in Dad's eyes.

"What were you doing this afternoon, Chris?"

"Oh, I don't know. I played ball, and then came home."

"Mr. Roberts tells me you broke the aerial of the car they had parked on the street. His wife saw you and told him when he got home. Is that true?" asked his dad.

Chris looked down, feeling hot with embarrassment. His foot traced a circle on the rug. Finally he nodded.

"Why, Chris? Why did you do it?" asked Dad.

The words choked in Chris's throat, but finally came. "I was mad," he said. "Mad at the ump. He didn't call the game fair, and we lost. He made it look like it was all my fault."

Chris stopped. He couldn't tell Dad all of it. He had been so mad he wanted to lash out at anything he could. It had been such an awful day, he wondered if anyone cared what happened to him.

"What do you think you should say to Mr. Roberts?" asked Dad.

Slowly Chris looked up. "I guess I should say I'm sorry." He really meant it, but felt so ashamed it didn't sound that way.

"I forgive you, but I think you should talk to my wife," said Mr. Roberts. "She uses that car for work."

Chris's feet dragged all the way to the Roberts's house. From the time he was a little kid he'd known

Mrs. Roberts. When he was five or six, he and the other kids often stopped there for cookies. That was a long time ago, and now Chris felt ashamed to look her in the eyes.

"I'm sorry," he said, stumbling over the words. "I'm sorry I broke your aerial. It was a stupid thing to do."

"I know you're sorry," said Mrs. Roberts. "And I forgive you."

Chris looked up. "You forgive me? You aren't mad?"

"Yes, I forgive you. And I'm not mad. I'm disappointed about what you did, but I'm not mad."

"How come?" Chris asked, then felt surprised he'd spoken the words.

"Because I've done wrong things in my own life," answered Mrs. Roberts. "Yet when I ask forgiveness, Jesus *does* forgive me. He not only forgives, He forgets about it."

"Forgets about it?"

"Sure. He loves me as though I've never done anything wrong."

Chris wasn't sure about this God stuff. He'd like to believe she was right, but a part of him still wondered, "How can God or anyone forget what I did?"

"Now," Mrs. Roberts interrupted his thoughts. "I believe you mean it when you ask forgiveness. And I forgive you. As far as I'm concerned, everything is wiped clean between us. It's as though nothing ever happened. Okay?"

"Okay!" answered Chris, filled with relief.

"But there's one more thing," said Mrs. Roberts. "When Jesus forgives us, He wants us to turn from what we've done wrong and live a different way. What do you think would be a good way to show that you want to live a different way? Not breaking aerials anymore?"

Chris was puzzled. It felt good to be forgiven. But he didn't know. . . . Suddenly an idea struck him.

"I guess I should pay for the aerial," he said slowly.

"It would help you remember you don't want to do the same thing again," agreed Mrs. Roberts. "But that's quite a bit of money. What would be a fair amount of work to make up for our needing to buy a new aerial?"

"Oh, brother!" thought Chris. He could sure think of things he'd rather do than work. Yet whether he liked it or not, he knew Mrs. Roberts was right.

Together they decided Chris would mow the Roberts's lawn once a week for four weeks. The next afternoon he was back, glad Mrs. Roberts had forgiven him. She even treated him like old times. Yet Chris wished he could go swimming with his friends. Making quick sweeps around the yard, he wondered if he could finish in time to join them.

Halfway through, Mrs. Roberts came out of the

house and tapped him on the shoulder. "That's not good enough," she said, pointing to the hunks of grass Chris had missed.

Chris felt anger well up within. The fact that she was right made things worse. But he didn't have any choice. Swinging the mower around, he went over the hunks.

As he started a new section, Chris glanced back where he'd been. To his surprise, the grass looked nice! When he'd mowed the entire lawn, he checked it again. This time he felt proud of the work he'd done. The yard looked great except for the ragged edges that needed trimming by hand.

Chris started to the door to tell Mrs. Roberts he was finished. Midway he stopped, thinking about the edges he'd left ragged. "I don't have to," he told himself. "She didn't tell me to do the trimming."

Then came a thought he couldn't push aside. "But she didn't have to forgive me."

For a moment longer Chris stood there, trying to decide. "Maybe I can still go swimming," he thought. Then he remembered last night—how ashamed he'd been, and how good it felt when Mrs. Roberts forgave him.

"It was like she gave me a present."

Finding the clippers, Chris trimmed around the flowerbeds.

As he headed for the house a second time, Mrs.

Roberts came out with a plate of cookies.

"Wow!" thought Chris. "Things really are okay again!"

TO TALK ABOUT

▶We won't feel good about ourselves if we need God's forgiveness or someone else's. How did Chris feel after he broke the aerial? When did that feeling change?

▶"Confessing our sins" means to say we're sorry for what we did. What words did Chris use to ask forgiveness?

▶What words did Mrs. Roberts use to offer Chris the gift of forgiveness? What reason did she give for forgiving him?

▶Mrs. Roberts also told Chris that because he asked for forgiveness and she gave it, everything was okay between them. Why was it important for Chris to know that?

▶How does God see us after we ask forgiveness and He gives it to us? What has happened to our sin? Who made that possible? How?

▶How did Chris show that he not only was sorry for what he did, but wanted to live a different way?

42

Everyone has sinned and is far away from God's saving presence. But by the free gift of God's grace all are put right with him through Christ Jesus, who sets them free. (Romans 3:23-24, GNB)

Jesus, I'm sorry about the wrong thing I did. (Tell Jesus what it was.) I ask Your forgiveness. Thank You that when I ask, You forgive me. Thanks that in Your eyes I'm a new kid!

43

YOU'RE MY FRIEND

Lori looked down. No matter which way she twisted her skirt, she just couldn't make it fit right. Even worse, the material was starting to fade from the many times it had been washed.

Hastily she stuffed her shorts and shoes into her backpack. Up to this year, she liked gym the best of any class. Now she was starting to hate this moment. It always made her realize the difference between her clothes and those of the other girls.

Across the bathroom, her friend Heather stood in front of a mirror. As Lori watched, Heather carefully brushed her hair until it hung smoothly down her back. But it wasn't Heather's silky hair that made Lori feel out of it. It was Heather's new designer jeans.

Heather turned, saw Lori watching, and grinned. "Ready to go?" Lori nodded. Pushing through the crowded halls, they started down the street toward home. Living only two doors apart, they'd walked to and from school together for years.

The spring sunshine reminded Lori of a long ago time. Suddenly she laughed.

"What's funny?" asked Heather.

"Do you remember the day I met you?"

Heather's smile lighted her whole face. "How could I forget? I'd set up a stand in front of our house, and I was selling. . . ."

"Mudpies!" they shouted together, laughing at the memory.

"I ran home and got a penny," said Lori.

"So you could buy one!" Heather finished.

"And you were smeared from head to toe with mud. It had even dried on your face."

Again Heather laughed. "But I was in business!"

Lori joined in her laughter, then was quiet. They'd been together so long that sometimes Lori took Heather for granted. Though they'd been best friends for years, something was changing.

Heather broke the silence. "Lori, is something wrong?"

"Uh-uh," answered Lori, not wanting to admit how she felt.

"Are you sure?"

"Yep, I'm sure," said Lori.

"You'd tell me if something was wrong?"

Lori looked down and started kicking a stone along the edge of the street. "I'd like to bring back the old days," she thought. "Sometimes I feel so far away from Heather." Yet she felt embarrassed to say anything.

"Remember how we always shared secrets?" asked Heather. "Even when I made only one penny on mudpies?"

Lori smiled, but the ache didn't leave her heart. "I'm afraid to tell her," she thought. "Maybe she won't like me anymore."

But Heather knew her too well. "Spill it, Lori," she said.

For a long moment Lori waited, trying to decide what to do. At last she spoke. "Well, did you know that my dad got laid off a year ago?"

Heather nodded.

"And he still hasn't found work. Mom and Dad don't say much, but they seem different—worried, I guess. Last week I asked if we'll be able to stay here. Dad said, 'We'll keep trying with what your mother makes.'"

"Oh, Lori, I'm so glad. I don't know what I'd do if you moved."

Heather's words gave Lori courage. Somehow she went on in spite of the lump in her throat. "But sometimes I don't feel like your friend anymore. We used to be alike, and now we're different."

"Different?"

When Lori didn't answer, Heather spoke again. "What do you mean?"

Lori's face felt hot, and she knew she must be blushing. She could barely get the words out. "Our clothes," she said.

"Ohhhhhh." Understanding came into Heather's eyes. "And that's why you've been acting funny lately?"

Lori nodded.

"But don't you know, clothes shouldn't make any difference between us."

Lori looked down, afraid Heather would see how she felt. "Doesn't it bother you to walk down the hall with me? To have kids see the way I look? My clothes are so old. . . ."

Lori choked on the words, hardly able to speak. "And you have new designer jeans."

Heather stopped right where she was. Lori had to stop too. "Is that all that's bothering you?"

Lori nodded slowly. "I don't look like the other kids anymore. There's no money for clothes."

For a long moment Heather was silent. When she spoke, she sounded as if she'd been thinking for some time. "Lori, what if you had designer jeans, and I didn't? How would you treat me?"

The question surprised Lori. Her gaze met Heather's. "It wouldn't make any difference."

Heather laughed. "What did you say?"

"That it wouldn't," Lori stopped, suddenly feeling foolish.

For a moment they walked on without speaking. Then Heather broke the silence. "I've got an idea," she said.

Lori looked at her and waited, afraid to hope.

TO TALK ABOUT

▶What idea do you think Heather had? How do you think she helped Lori with her problem? What would you tell Lori to make her feel better?

▶How did Heather help Lori believe her worth as a person didn't depend on clothes?

▶Heather showed she was a true friend by asking Lori what was wrong. What would have happened if Lori hadn't told her?

▶Both Heather and Lori discovered something important about clothes. What did Heather have to know how to handle? What did Lori?

▶Why does it seem important to dress the same way other kids do? Have there been times when you felt embarrassed because your clothes weren't the same? What did you do about it?

▶What if a friend *didn't* ask what was bothering you, or try to help? How would it hurt your self-esteem?

▶Why would it be important for you to try to tell one of your friends that something was wrong?

The LORD does not look at the things man looks at. Man looks at the outward appearance, but the LORD looks at the heart (1 Samuel 16:7)

Help me, Lord, to look my best with what I have. But keep me from thinking I'm worth something only if I have the right clothes. I want to please You with the way I look on the inside.

ANGELO CARRIES THE PIGSKIN

Angelo gripped the football, lifted it behind his ear, and took one step ahead. With a snap of the wrist he sent a long pass to Dad.

"Great!" Dad called out with approval. "Now let me show you a trick play."

Angelo liked playing football with Dad. He knew it gave him an advantage over many of the boys. Yet sometimes. . . .

Dad moved closer. "You can teach this to Joey, and do it together. You grip the ball, hold it behind your head as if you're going to pass. Like this, see?"

Angelo watched.

"As I hold the ball, you run up behind and take it."

Angelo moved out. Running hard, he grabbed the

ball from Dad's hands and kept going.

"Now, try it the other way," said Dad. "Pretend you're going to pass. I'll take it off you."

With split-second timing, Angelo lifted the pigskin. Dad grabbed it and kept going.

"Attaboy!" shouted Dad.

Dad's praise warmed Angelo. He knew he was getting better all the time. He also knew he had the build to become a good player. If only. . . .

Dad slapped him across the shoulders. "You're just a chip off the old block."

"That's what bothers me," thought Angelo. "What if I can't do as well as Dad did?"

"You'll be just as good a player as I was—better!" said Dad, as though reading his thoughts. "If I hadn't hurt my knee, I'd have made it to the big time."

"There it is again," thought Angelo. "He wants *me* to make it there. What if I'm not good enough?"

That afternoon the question stayed with Angelo during the ride to the football field. Like a long-ago dream, he remembered how he used to look forward to playing football. Somehow it wasn't fun anymore. He wondered if the Lions would be too much for them.

As he walked onto the field, Angelo offered his usual prayer, asking God to help him play a good game. Today he added a request. "So Dad likes what I do, God."

Yet at the half the Bears were one point behind

the Lions. With minutes left to play, Angelo glanced at the sidelines and saw Dad's tense face.

In the huddle Angelo told Joey and the coach about the trick play.

The coach nodded. "It's a good one. I've used it. Let's try it on the next play and see if we can recover. Angelo, take left back. Pick up the ball from Joey and try for the right end. They've got a weak man there."

The whistle blew. Both teams fell into line. Above the cheering crowd, Angelo picked out Dad's voice. "Go for it, Angelo!" He wished Dad wouldn't shout louder than the rest.

As Angelo watched, Joey took his position as quarterback. Muscles tense, Angelo crouched.

The ball snapped into Joey's hands. Gripping the pigskin, he faded back. Holding it up behind his head, he looked as though he were going to pass. In that instant Angelo moved forward, grabbed the ball, and started around the right end.

He'd almost made it when he sensed someone coming up from his left. Twisting, he zigzagged. Knees high, he cleared the other team, running fast.

The crowd roared. "Twenty yards to go," he thought, the pressure mounting within him.

Just then he heard Dad's voice. "He's coming up, Angelo! Pour it on!"

Angelo turned his head and stumbled. In that instant he lost his timing. A second later he crashed to

the ground. The ball popped out of his hands.

Rolling over, Angelo tried to recover, but a Lion tackle landed on the ball. Three minutes later the final whistle blew. The Bears had lost.

Angelo felt sick inside. "I would have made it. If I hadn't heard Dad and turned, I would have made it."

Shoulders slumped, he climbed into the car, dreading the ride home. He didn't need to look at Dad. Angelo knew he'd be mad.

"You had it in the bag, Angelo. What was the matter with you?" asked Dad.

Angelo picked out a spot on the dashboard and stared straight ahead.

"You know better than to look around. I've told you a hundred times!"

Still Angelo didn't answer, but his anger felt like a river rushing toward a dam. "I just can't be Dad," he thought. "And I can't tell him how I feel. It'd be easier to quit playing football."

The car stopped, and Angelo got out. All he could think about was how much fun it used to be to play with Joey.

TO TALK ABOUT

▶ How did Angelo feel about losing the game? Why is it important that he lets his dad know how he feels?
▶ What could Dad say to Angelo to help him become

an in-spite-of-it kid? How can he help Angelo enjoy football again?

▶ Angelo's dad helped him learn important football skills. What's the difference between a parent helping a son or daughter learn important skills and pushing them to live out a dream? At what point did Angelo start feeling pushed?

▶ Is there some area of your life where you feel pushed beyond what you can do? How is that different from pushing yourself enough to learn how to do something well?

▶ If Angelo keeps playing, but doesn't tell his dad what's wrong, how will it affect his life and his relationship with his dad?

I run in the path of your commands, for you have set my heart free. (Psalm 119:32)

Help me, Jesus, to learn the things You want me to learn, but to talk about the things I can't handle. Thank You that I'm valuable to You just the way I am.

CHRISTMAS LOVE

As the kids at school talked, Joanna wanted to put her hands over her ears. She wanted to shut out the sound. But the voices sounded like hammers pounding on steel.

"Your mom dropped you on a doorstep," said one of the girls.

"She didn't want you," added another.

As soon as she could get away, Joanna took off. When she was out of the kids' sight, she began running for home. By the time she reached the front door she was panting. Taking a deep breath, she quietly slipped inside.

"Maybe I can get to my bedroom without anyone seeing me," she thought.

But the little Christmas bells on the door gave Joanna away. As she tiptoed toward the steps, Mom came into the hall.

"Joanna! Where have you been?" she asked.

Joanna kept moving, but as she passed under the light, Mom stopped her.

"What's the matter?" Mom asked gently.

Joanna wondered if her cheeks were streaked from crying. "Nothing," she said.

"You can tell me, you know," answered Mom.

"I said *nothing*," snapped Joanna, the hurt within her changing to anger. "I mean nothing."

But Mom put an arm around her shoulder. "Dad's home, and we've been putting up the tree. Come and see."

Knowing there was no escape, Joanna walked slowly into the family room. The tree was beautiful, the tallest she could remember. Dad stood on a chair, putting lights on the branches near the top. Seeing Joanna, he climbed down to give her a hug.

"Have a hard day?" he asked.

Joanna shrugged. She didn't want to say what was wrong. But as Dad gave her another hug, the words tumbled out.

"The kids at school said I was adopted."

Joanna saw the look that passed between Mom and Dad, but it was Dad who spoke first.

"You know that. We've talked about it with you

lots of times. Why is it bothering you now?"

"One of the kids heard her mom talking about me. She said my mother didn't want me, and that's why you adopted me."

Joanna's shoulders began to shake. "She said my mom dropped me on a doorstep. My own *mother* didn't want me. I wasn't worth anything, not even to her. I'm just—just. . . ."

Joanna broke off, and plopped into Dad's big chair. "I'm just a big zero!" she wailed.

Dad sat down on the floor, cross-legged, in front of her. Mom pulled up a chair beside him. Joanna's sobs increased. She needed to know someone loved her. But she didn't know how to say it, or how to ask all the things she wanted to know.

As she blew her nose, Dad spoke. "Joanna, do you remember what we've told you about your birth mother?" he asked.

Joanna nodded her head, and Dad went on.

"We know your mother was only fourteen when you were born. And it's true that she left you on a doorstep. But social workers found out who she was. They told us she would've had a hard time taking care of you. She didn't have any way to give you a good home."

Mom reached forward and gently pushed the hair out of Joanna's eyes. "Do you remember your first doll?"

Joanna nodded.

"Everywhere you went you took that doll," said Mom. "You wanted to hug it and hang onto it. We learned that your mother felt that way about you. She wanted to keep you. It hurt her to give you up."

"You were very special to her," said Dad. "But she let go of her own wishes. She believed someone else would give you a better life."

Joanna sat up and searched Dad's face. "But the kids said she didn't *want* to keep me—that she didn't *want* to be my mother."

"She *did* want to," said Dad. "She let you be adopted because she wanted to give you the best opportunity to be happy."

Joanna drew a deep breath. "That's really true?"

"Really true," echoed Dad. "And we wanted you. We chose to have you."

"But you didn't know me," answered Joanna. "I was just a little baby. You didn't know what I'd be like."

"We prayed about you," said Dad. "We believed that no matter what you'd be like, God wanted you to be part of our family."

Dad grinned. "And we got the best end of the deal!"

Joanna looked into Dad's eyes. Again she searched his face. Something warm stirred inside her, a feeling that Dad really meant what he said.

She thought about it for a moment, letting the

feeling sink in. Then another thought struck her. "I'm twelve, and my mom was fourteen when she had me."

The idea of taking care of a baby all the time scared Joanna. She wondered if that was how her birth mother felt.

Just then Mom spoke. "Joanna, Dad and I love you. I think you're forgetting why we gave you your name. Remember what it means?"

"God is gracious," answered Joanna.

"Right," Mom said. "That means God is kind. You're our special gift from Him."

This time it was Mom who had tears in her eyes. "Joanna, we don't know yet how it will affect your life that you lived with us instead of your birth mother. But as you grow up, let God show you good things about it."

As the tears brimmed over onto Mom's cheeks, Joanna crawled out of Dad's chair. This time it was Joanna who gave the hugs.

TO TALK ABOUT

▶ To be rejected means to be unwanted. When Joanna thought her birth mother didn't want her, how did she feel about herself?

▶ In what ways did Joanna's adoptive parents show their love? How did they help Joanna know she was special to them?

61

▶ Every one of us needs to know we're loved just the way we are. Do you wonder if you're loved? Why is it important to talk to your mom or dad about it?

▶ Do you know someone who is adopted? How has it changed that person's life?

▶ Have you been adopted? What questions do you have that you've never asked your adoptive parents?

Those who trust in the LORD are protected by his constant love. (Psalm 32:10, GNB)

Thank You, Jesus, that no matter what happens to me, I can turn to You. But when I have questions, help me talk about them. Help me know I'm worth something—even a lot! Thank You for loving me at all times.

AFTER THE PLAY

The high school play needed some younger boys, and Tony and three of his friends were chosen. Being in the cast was the most fun he'd had in a long time.

Now the curtain fell on their last performance, then swept open again. Together the cast ran onto the stage. As they took their final bows, the applause grew. Here and there people rose from their seats. Others joined in a standing ovation.

"Wow!" thought Tony. "They really liked it. Guess it was worth all the work!"

As the curtain closed around them, his friend Dustin found him in the crowd. "Hey, Tony, we're having a party."

"You mean with the juniors and seniors?"

"Nah, our own party. I've asked a bunch of kids, and they're asking their friends. We'll meet at my house. Have your mom and dad drop you off."

Tony felt torn. One part of him thought, "I want to go. It should be fun." The other part wondered, "What kind of a party will it be?"

He knew why they'd go to Dustin's. His parents hadn't come to the play, and they wouldn't be at home either. They were always out somewhere.

The thought made Tony uncomfortable, but he still wanted to go. "Maybe I can be a witness for Jesus to them," he told himself.

Forty-five minutes later Tony and his friend Joel stood on Dustin's front step. Through the closed door and windows, the beat of a strong bass rose and fell. Tony pounded on the door. When no one heard them, he and Joel walked in.

Dustin met them on the stairs to the basement. "Hey, guys! Glad you could make it. There's food on the bar."

"All riiiiight!" Tony was hungry. He took the steps in a bound and found the room full of kids.

"Hi, Tony!" called out one after another. "Good show!" said many. "You were great!" By the time he reached the bar, Tony felt warmed by their praise.

With the music thumping around him, he heaped his plate with food. "What a night!" he thought as his feelings soared. "First the play, now this."

But a moment later he crashed to earth. Dustin entered the room with two six-packs of beer in his hands.

Someone turned down the music. Dustin stood on a chair, holding high a can of beer. "Let's give a toast for the best play this side of Chicago!"

A cheer went up. Another boy grabbed a can, raising it above his head. "And let's give a toast to the best girls in the state!"

Setting down his food, Tony glanced at Joel. Joel looked just as uncomfortable as Tony felt.

Tony worked his way over to Dustin. "Hey, where'd you get the beer?"

"My older brother bought it for us. What's the matter? What's it to you?"

"You know we're breaking the law."

"So? Big deal."

"What if our parents or the cops find out? We'll be in big trouble."

"Who's gonna give us away? You and Joel are the only guys who might squeal."

Tony looked around and knew Dustin was right. Then another idea struck him. "What if a neighbor complains about the noise?"

"They never do," Dustin answered. "Forget it."

In that moment, Tony knew he'd been fooling only one person. "Be a witness here?" he asked himself.

"What a laugh."

Dustin began throwing beer cans to the kids around the room. Someone cranked up the stereo again.

Tony edged over to Joel. "I don't like this. Let's get out of here."

The music beating around him, Tony bounded up the steps and out the front door. Joel followed him.

Once outside, Tony breathed deep. "Want some burgers?" he asked Joel. Together they headed off down the street.

TO TALK ABOUT

▶ Do you believe Tony really thought he would witness for Jesus at the party? Why do you think that?

▶ If you were Tony, how would you feel about being at Dustin's party? How can feeling awkward in a group sometimes protect you?

▶ In leaving the party, Tony made a choice. What do you think happened after he and Joel left? What do you suppose Dustin said to Tony the next time they saw each other?

▶ Have there been times when you refused to go along with something other kids were doing? What happened? How did you feel about yourself afterward?

▶ Kids who have a strong self-esteem are able to do what's right in spite of what other kids think. Not feeling a part of some groups isn't bad. Why is it important to know when it's time to leave a place? ▶When you hurt because of what kids think about you, what can help you feel better? Whose opinion of you matters the most?

Flee the evil desires of youth, and pursue righteousness, faith, love and peace, along with those who call on the Lord out of a pure heart (2 Timothy 2:22)

Jesus, when I get mixed up in something wrong, I'm often afraid to do the right thing. In those times, show me what to do. Then give me the Holy Spirit's power to do it. Thank You!

NIKKI LOOKS IN THE MIRROR

As they began to sing, Nikki leaned forward to watch the excitement on Cindy's face.

"Happy birthday to you—Happy birthday to you—Happy birthday, dear Cindy. . . ."

For a moment Cindy waited, deciding about her wish. Then with a mighty whoooof she blew out every candle.

The girls clapped. "Yaaaaay, Cindy!"

The party had been fun. As Cindy's mom cut the cake, Nikki looked from face to face. Several girls were laughing. One was ready to pop a balloon. Close by, Nikki saw the heads of two girls reflected in a mirror. Then she saw herself.

"Ugh," she thought. Turning, she leaned closer to the mirror. "I look just awful. The zits on my nose get worse every day."

Glancing back to the group around the table, she looked at each girl's nose. "Not anyone—not a single person—has zits as bad as mine," she thought. "How can anyone possibly like me when my skin is so awful?"

Restlessly, Nikki stretched out her feet under the table. As she bumped something, she saw the girl next to her jump. Nikki turned and realized she must have hit the brace on April's leg. "Oh, I'm sorry," she said. "Did I hurt you?"

April smiled. "No, I'm okay. Don't worry about it." She moved her leg, then bent down and pushed her crutches farther beneath her chair.

Soon the party was over, and all the girls clustered around Cindy's bed to pick up their coats. Once again Nikki caught sight of herself in a mirror. "What can I do?" she thought. "How can I hide my zits?"

She shrugged into her coat, thanked Cindy's mom, and went outside. During the party, the dropping temperature had changed light rain to sleet. Ice coated the sidewalk. Ahead of Nikki, one of the girls took a flying run. "Wheeee! Race you!" she called out.

Nikki followed in a long slide. Feeling the wind against her face, she wished her mixed-up feelings could blow right out of her head.

She felt glad no one's parents had known it was icy and come to pick them up. Often she liked walking home after a party, talking all the way, best of all. But now, though she wanted to be with the others, she wondered, "Will they notice my fresh crop of zits?"

As she joined her two closest friends, Nikki glanced back at Cindy's house. Just then April came out the front door, arms encircled by the leather rings at the top of her crutches. "Always the last," thought Nikki. "Always takes her longer."

All at once she realized April wouldn't know it had turned icy. In that moment, April set her crutches ahead and started slowly down the steps, her brace glinting under the porch light. Suddenly she slid. Panic stiffened her face. Reaching out, she caught the rail just in time.

With a bound Nikki was by her side. "Here, let me help you," she said.

"No, no, I'm okay," answered April, sounding as if she was still scared.

"The sidewalk's icy too," said Nikki. She slid her hand under April's arm. "How could I be so self-centered?" she wondered. "Thinking I'm nothing because I have zits, when April can barely walk?"

Her grip tightened on April's arm. "Let me help you," she repeated.

"Thanks," said April, "but I'll be okay. You go ahead. They're waiting for you."

Nikki's friends had stopped. "Hey, hurry up," they called.

Nikki wanted to join them. Besides, April would go the opposite direction. Not only would she have to walk to April's condo, she'd have to come all the way back again.

"What should I do?" Nikki wondered. "Help April home? Or go with my friends? I'd much rather be with them."

TO TALK ABOUT

▶What do you think was worse—Nikki's zits or how she felt about them?

▶When did Nikki's feelings of worthlessness change? How do you know?

▶When Nikki hurried to help April, she chose between feeling sorry for herself and thinking about someone else. Are there some ways in which you're feeling sorry for yourself? What can you think about instead?

▶When you make a choice to think about and meet the needs of others, how do you end up feeling about yourself?

▶April also had a choice to make. She could go back inside to phone for a ride, or she could try walking home. Why do you think April wanted to walk home instead of asking for help?

Don't just think about your own affairs, but be interested in others, too, and in what they are doing.
(Philippians 2:4, TLB)

Forgive me, Lord, for thinking so much about myself that I forget about the needs of others. Help me to be aware of ways other people need help. Then give me a heart that's willing to reach out. Thank You, Jesus.

MESS IN THE GARAGE

A wave of hopelessness swept over Jerry as he looked around the garage. Someone had left the door open, and a neighborhood dog got in. Before being discovered, he'd tipped over two garbage cans and emptied them on the floor.

A large mound of firewood cluttered the other side of the garage. Rakes and shovels leaned against the wall. Dad's workbench looked like it had been struck by a tornado.

"Do we really have to clean it all up?" Jerry asked.

Mom nodded. "A lot of it is stuff you and Doug haven't put away. I want you to work together."

Jerry groaned. "Spend my Saturday this way?" he thought.

But Mom went on. "Dad's really tired. He doesn't have enough help at the store right now. He'll work all day, just trying to catch up."

Jerry's older brother Doug stood there, looking at the mess. If he felt as overwhelmed as Jerry, Doug didn't say anything.

Mom turned to him. "I'll be at church until about one, fixing food for the funeral. When I come back, I want to see this done."

Again it was Jerry who spoke up. "I don't know what to do with all this junk."

"Take one thing at a time. Dad threw the wood inside so it wouldn't get rained on. Stack it along that wall," she said, pointing to a far corner. "If both of you just keep going, you'll be surprised how quickly you'll be done."

She blew them both a kiss and headed for the car.

Jerry started with the firewood. "Dumb old stuff!" he thought. It was hard to remember how much he liked to lie in front of the fire in winter. On this sunny October day he wanted to be outside, riding his bike or playing football.

All the wood was split and ready to stack. With a thump! bang! Jerry threw it against the wall. But it wasn't long before he knew that throwing the wood wasn't going to work.

When one side of the stack tumbled down, he turned the logs on the end a different direction. With

that end braced, the other end held firmly against the wall. Then Jerry restacked the falling pieces.

Standing back to look at what he'd done, he felt good. The pile looked solid and straight. After working all day at his hardware store, Dad would be pleased.

But the garage seemed awfully quiet. Jerry looked around. "Where's Doug?" he wondered.

Going to a window of the house, Jerry yelled inside to him.

"I'm getting a broom," Doug shouted back.

Jerry returned to the garage. Taking a stepladder, he pounded long nails into the wall and hung up the shovels and rakes. But when he finished, Doug still wasn't there.

77

Once again Jerry went to the window and called.

"I'm still looking for the broom!" Doug yelled back.

Jerry sat down on a stump outside the garage. He was getting mad. "I'm not gonna work if he doesn't," he thought. For a long time he sat there, wishing he could take off on his bike.

Finally he decided he didn't want to waste the whole day. "I'll get my half done, and Doug can finish the rest."

This time he started on Dad's workbench. Before long, he had all the tools put away, each on its own peg. Again Jerry felt good inside. But as he looked around, he knew he'd done more than half the work. He thought about Doug not helping and felt mad all the way through.

This time Jerry crept quietly into the house. There was Doug, lying on the floor in front of the TV!

Seeing Jerry, Doug jumped up. "I just found the broom."

"Sure!" said Jerry. "And I did every bit of the work!"

"Well, good!" said Doug. "So we're all done?"

Jerry wanted to belt him one, but Doug was bigger. "I'm sure not gonna do any more. All that's left are the two garbage cans and sweeping the floor. If you don't do it, I'll tell Mom."

"Ha, ha, ha, ha, ha," Doug answered in a singsong chant. "What are you, a Mama's boy?"

Jerry grabbed the broom and went after Doug. But Doug pulled it from him and sauntered out to the garage.

So mad he wanted to throw something, Jerry grabbed an apple and chomped on it furiously. Then he went to the garage for his bike.

Doug had picked up the stuff from the two garbage cans and started sweeping the floor. Seeing Jerry, he waved the broom and smirked.

Grabbing his bike, Jerry hopped on and pedaled out of the garage. Just then Mom drove up.

"Wow!" she said, seeing the garage, and Doug sweeping the floor. "It's great the way you put everything away. Doug, you really did a nice job. I'm proud of you."

Then she looked at Jerry, ready to pedal off. "Where are you going, young man? The work's not done."

"Hey, Mom," he started. "I . . . . ."

"Yeh, Jerry, come here," interrupted Doug. "Finish sweeping the floor."

"Mommmm," Jerry started again. "I did more than half!"

Before Jerry could explain, Doug jumped in again. "Hey, little brother. Don't start making up stories!"

Mom just looked from one to the other.

"Believe me, Mom," Jerry pleaded. Something inside him crumpled. All that work, and. . . .

Again Doug interrupted him. "You liar!"

Once again Mom looked from Jerry to Doug. "Stop it! I've had a hard day with the funeral and all. I can't handle your fighting right now. Finish this up, okay?"

Slowly she walked to the house. Without speaking, Jerry looked after her. Then he looked around the garage. In the corner the wood was neatly stacked. The workbench was clear and ready for Dad to use. Along the wall hung the rakes and shovels. But Doug would get the credit.

Inside, Jerry didn't feel good anymore. In fact, he felt mad. Then he thought more about it. What was more important? Getting credit? Or helping Dad?

Finally he shrugged. "Oh well," he told himself. "It feels good to help Dad when he's so busy. Let Doug take the credit if he wants it that badly."

Climbing on his bike, he pedaled off to the playground.

TO TALK ABOUT

▶ When his mom feels ready to talk again, what do you think Jerry should say to her?

▶ If Jerry has been a good worker before, she'll probably believe his story. If he hasn't been a good worker, she might not. What do you think will happen?

▶ Have you ever worked hard to do something and not gotten credit for it? How did you feel? How did it hurt your self-esteem?

▶ If Jerry doesn't get credit for doing most of the work, he could stay mad and spend the rest of his life saying, "It wasn't fair." Some things in life *aren't* fair. But there's something else Jerry can choose to remember. What do you think that might be?

"You have been faithful with a few things; I will put you in charge of many things." (Matthew 25:21)

Jesus, I hurt inside when someone else gets the credit for something I did well. Please help me sort out my feelings. Thank You that You see everything I do and give me the credit I deserve.

81

CATHY'S SONG

Minutes before the spring concert started, Cathy's stomach fluttered. Behind her on the stage of the school auditorium, the band was warming up. Tuning notes and runs blended in a swirl of sound.

As the choir formed lines backstage, Cathy edged over to the side of the closed curtain. Through the narrow space between the cloth and the wall, she could see half the audience. By now most of the seats were filled.

Starting at the front, she checked each row. As she came to the last one, she sighed. "They're not here," she thought. "Neither Mom nor Dad came."

Just to be sure, Cathy crossed the stage to the

other side of the curtain. Her friend Lyn joined her.

"Just a minute. Let me look," said Lyn, peering over Cathy's shoulder. "Yep! There they are! Right in the front row."

Cathy looked too. Sure enough, there was Lyn's family—her mom and dad, all three sisters, a brother, and a grandmother. "And she's not even singing a solo!" Cathy thought, feeling even more alone.

"Did you find your parents?" said Lyn.

Cathy shook her head, and tried to swallow around the lump in her throat. Lyn's parents had given her a ride to school so she could be there early. But Mom promised she and Dad would come in time for the concert.

"Will they really?" Cathy wondered. "That's what they said last time. And the time before. And the time before that."

Once again Cathy peered through the crack on the side of the curtain, checking the audience. Starting at the front, she looked across each row. The farther back she went, the more desperate she felt. She was afraid to come to that last row and know they weren't there.

"See 'em?" asked Lyn.

Cathy shook her head numbly. She wished she could tell Lyn how she felt. She wished Lyn would hug her and say it was okay. But during the winter concert Dad had been out of town on business. Mom was busy

84

at church. Would they be too busy again?

Cathy sighed, the despair within her growing.

Lyn tugged her arm. "Come on. We have to get in line."

Following Lyn, Cathy found her place in the choir. Her shoulders sagged. "Do they really love me?" she wondered. "Do Mom and Dad love me enough to be here?"

"Maybe they'll still come," Lyn said softly.

"The choir's first and the band's second," Cathy whispered back. "My solo's in the fourth song. I've practiced two whole months, and no one will hear me!"

"I will," said Lyn, gripping her hand.

Cathy wasn't able to smile. "How can I sing when I just want to cry?" she thought.

Just then the curtain opened, and Cathy followed the line of singers onto the risers that faced the audience. In the brief moments before she looked at the director, Cathy's eyes searched the rows once more. Mom and Dad still weren't there.

During the first song, she sang through stiff lips. All the way through, Cathy felt mad.

Halfway into the next number, she felt sorry for herself. She wished she belonged to Lyn's family. As a tear slid down her cheek, Cathy froze like a statue, trying to pretend nothing was wrong.

Just before the choir started the third number,

she straightened her shoulders and cleared her throat. Singing always made her feel better. Maybe no one else would understand how the music seemed to swell up within her. "But I'm gonna do the best I can," she thought.

Her solo was next. Stepping out of the choir, Cathy moved forward to the microphone. All she could think about were the words she needed to remember. As she listened to the piano introduction, she saw the lift of Mr. Lee's baton.

Cathy began to sing, and her first notes wavered. Then her voice grew stronger. As she reached for the high notes, she knew it was the best she'd ever sung. In that moment she forgot everything that was troubling her. She just felt the music.

When the applause broke around her, Cathy smiled and bowed. But she looked in only one direction. Toward the back.

TO TALK ABOUT

▶ What do you think Cathy saw at the back of the auditorium? How do you think she felt?

▶ God loves and cares for each of us. But why do we need to know we're loved by the people we love?

▶ What happened when Cathy decided she wasn't going to feel sorry for herself? How did she become an in-spite-of-it kid?

▶How have you been disappointed by someone you love? Were you able to straighten it out? How?
▶There is one *Person* who wants to always be with you—Jesus. There is one *thing* that will never change—His love for you. What does it mean to say, "Jesus is with me"? How can you *know* that, even though you don't *feel* it?

Jesus said, "You will not be left all alone; I will come back to you." (John 14:18, GNB)

When I feel all alone, help me, Jesus, to know You are with me. Help me to also know Your love through my Mom or Dad, or someone else important to me. Thank You!

I CAN'T HELP WONDERING

Todd was upstairs and not quite ready to leave when he heard the doorbell ring. A moment later Mom answered it. Todd heard the low rumble of his dad's voice.

Taking a final swipe at his hair, he moved quietly to the top of the stairs. Sure enough, they were arguing. Now and then Todd heard his name. "It must be about me," he thought.

Walking on tiptoe, he went back to his room. He'd already been in the middle of too many fights. He didn't want it to happen again.

His back against the door, Todd stood there clenching and unclenching his fists. He dreaded going downstairs. He wished it could be like the old days, when Dad lived here, and all of them did things together.

Then the same old question popped into Todd's mind. He tried to push it aside, but it didn't leave. Instead, he felt tears in his eyes. He blinked, wishing they'd go away, but they stayed.

Just then a knock came on his door. "Todddd," called his mom.

Todd wiped his eyes, grabbed his jacket, and opened the door. Mom stood in the hall with a bright smile on her face. As usual, she acted as though nothing had happened. Todd wished he could make everything all right for her.

"Your dad's here," she said. "Have a good time."

After a quick goodbye hug, Todd was down the stairs and out the door. Climbing into the car, he wished he could know Dad the way he used to, instead of just across a table in a restaurant.

Then the question returned. Todd pushed it to the back of his mind and pretended the answer didn't really matter.

But it did. Somehow Todd felt lonely for his dad, even though he sat right next to him.

In the restaurant Dad started out the usual way, "Order whatever you want, Son."

Todd asked for his usual hamburger, and Dad got his usual steak. But nothing seemed usual between them.

Todd wanted to blurt out everything that had happened that week, but didn't know where to start. When Dad asked, "What have you been doing?" he answered, "Oh, nothing."

When Dad told about his business trip to New York, Todd wanted to hear about the Statue of Liberty. But the questions stuck in his throat and he gave up.

Then Dad asked, "How's your chess club?" and Todd forgot to tell him about the good move he'd discovered. All he wanted to know was why Dad and Mom argued about him again.

As Todd finished his hamburger, Dad brought up his news. "I talked with your mom about taking you camping for a week," he said. "I want to go up in the mountains. I'll teach you to backpack and fish."

"Wow! Really?" asked Todd, hardly able to believe his ears.

"Really! Want to go?"

For Todd it was a dream come true. Camping. Fishing the trout streams. Being with Dad for a whole week.

But then the question came back again, and Todd felt shaky inside. Suddenly he couldn't stand it any longer. "Dad. . . ."

Todd's tongue felt as though it were clumsy with peanut butter, but the question didn't go away. It must have stayed on his face.

"What's the matter, Son?" Dad asked.

91

Then the peanut butter disappeared, and Todd's words tumbled out, as though he couldn't stop them. "Do you *really* want to take me with you?"

"Of course I want to take you with me," said Dad. "Why do you ask?"

Again Todd struggled to speak. But it was something he had to know.

"Do you really want me along? Or are you just trying to get me away from Mom?"

Dad looked startled. "Todd, what a strange question."

Todd looked down and began kicking his feet against the table.

For a moment Dad was silent. When he spoke his words came out slowly. "Don't you know how much I love you?"

Todd blinked, afraid the tears would return.

"Why do you wonder about it?" asked Dad, his voice quiet.

Staring at his water glass, Todd twisted it around in circles. At last he got the words out. "Because you and Mom fight about me all the time."

"Ohhhhhh," Dad's voice was so strange that Todd looked up. His face looked even stranger.

Finally Dad drew a long breath. "Todd, I'm sorry to say it, but your mother and I seem to disagree about everything. Whether you're around or not wouldn't make any difference. We'd probably argue anyway."

Dad cleared his throat. "I'm not proud of it. I'm sorry we act that way. But that's our problem, not yours."

As Dad grew silent, Todd's gaze fell. Once again he began twisting his glass. "He didn't answer my question," he thought. "Does he really want me? Does he like me the way I am? I can't help wondering." Todd had to know, but he couldn't ask the question again.

After a long moment, Dad spoke. "Want to see something?" Dad opened his wallet to pictures of Todd from the time he was a little kid. "I carry these around all the time. That way I can look at you whenever I want."

Inside, Todd felt a glimmer of hope.

"Today your mom and I had a discussion because I want to take you camping," said Dad. "I'm not just trying to get you away from your mom. You mean so much to me that I want you with me."

Todd looked up and searched Dad's face. What he found there made him feel good all over.

Todd knew Dad meant what he said.

TO TALK ABOUT

▶What was the question Todd wanted to ask?
▶Todd made a choice, whether to ask the question or keep wondering. Why was it important to his self-esteem to find out the truth?

▶How do you know Todd's mom and dad wanted to do the best they could for him?

▶Todd had been bottling up his feelings instead of telling his mom and dad what bothered him. What does it mean to "bottle up your feelings"? Why is it important to tell your feelings to someone who will listen and help?

▶When you need to talk about things that hurt you, it helps to start by saying, "I feel (bad, sorry, hurt, etc.) and finish the sentence. Todd could have told his dad, "I feel bad because you and Mom argue about me." Is there something bothering you that you'd like to talk about? Try starting with "I feel" and finish the sentence.

Thoughtless words can wound as deeply as any sword, but wisely spoken words can heal. (Proverbs 12:18, GNB)

Help me, Jesus, when I need to talk and ask questions about what's happening to me. When I feel bad about something, give me Your healing. Give me people who say things that will help. And help me remember You're always there to listen and understand.

94

WHAT SHOULD I DO?

For a long time Janie had wanted to be friends with Sheila. Sheila told funny stories. She seemed sure of herself. She and the girls who hung around with her always seemed to have something to do.

Janie, on the other hand, felt lonely. She didn't have any close friends. Every day felt the same.

"What could I do to make Sheila like me?" thought Janie. More than once she had asked herself that question. So far she hadn't come up with any answer.

Then one July morning, as Janie was on her way to the grocery store for Mom, Sheila caught up with her. "Where you going?" she asked.

Janie felt glad Sheila wanted to talk. It didn't

sound very exciting to pick up a gallon of milk, but that didn't seem to bother Sheila. "If you're headed that way, let's get an ice cream cone."

That was another thing Janie had noticed about Sheila. She always seemed to have money. Just last week Sheila had worn a new blouse.

A few days later Janie met Sheila's friend Colleen. Janie had been right—Sheila *did* think of things to do. But now and then she said things Janie didn't understand. Sheila and Colleen would laugh, and Janie didn't understand why. It made her uneasy. But most of the time, she liked being with them. Best of all, she started to feel she belonged.

Then one hot afternoon, Sheila gave Janie a call. "Wanna do something?"

"What're you gonna do?" Janie asked.

For the first time Sheila sounded as if she didn't have a plan. "Oh, I don't know," she said. "We'll find something. Meet you outside the ice cream store, okay?"

For some reason Janie felt uneasy, the way she had when Sheila and Colleen laughed. But Janie pushed it to the back of her mind, feeling glad she'd been asked to go.

"Colleen needs a new swimsuit," said Sheila when they met.

There was only one place to go for that—The Fashion Rack. As they left the hot sidewalk for the cool store, Sheila moved closer to Janie. "Colleen doesn't have enough money for the swimsuit," she said in a low voice. "We're gonna help her out."

"What do you mean?" asked Janie. "I don't have much money either."

"That's not what I'm saying." Sheila sounded as though she thought Janie wasn't very smart.

Startled, Janie looked at her. "Hey, count me out." She turned, ready to head out the door.

"Not so fast," said Sheila. "You like being along, don't you? Stick with us, and you'll have lots of fun."

Janie knew that was true. Already she'd had good times with Sheila and her friends.

"Tell you what," said Sheila. "Instead of getting a swimsuit for Colleen, let's get something for you today. What do you want?"

Again Janie looked at her, not liking what she heard. That wasn't her way of thinking. She seldom got things she wanted, only what she needed. And she didn't go into a store thinking, "This is what I'm going to take."

"What do I want?" she asked.

"Sure," said Sheila, still in a low voice. "What do you want? Look around."

"Well," thought Janie. "It won't hurt to look. But I won't take anything."

The girls spread out, moving throughout the store. Janie started at a rack of jackets. Sure enough, there was just the jacket she'd like to have. She glanced at the price tag, and knew that was out.

From there she went to the jeans. She hadn't bought a pair in a long time. "Maybe I deserve them," she thought.

She pushed away the idea, wishing it hadn't entered her head. But at the next rack she saw a blouse just like the one Sheila wore last week. "I wonder. . . ."

Janie didn't finish the idea, even to herself.

A moment later Sheila was at her side. "Everybody does it," she said, as though there'd been no break in the conversation. "You wanna be like the rest of us, don't you?"

"Sure," thought Janie, then hated herself for the thought.

Sheila moved closer and lowered her voice. "I'll tell you how."

As a clerk walked over, Sheila turned to her. "Right now we're just looking," she said.

The clerk moved away, and Sheila began talking again. Soon Janie knew the plan. She felt scared inside, but listened, knowing she wouldn't really do what Sheila said.

Sheila started edging away. "I'll give you the signal."

"Hey, wait," said Janie. Now she was more than scared. A tug-of-war battled inside. One part of her wanted the blouse. The other part knew it was wrong.

"I'd have to save a long time to get it with my allowance," she told herself.

From three racks away Sheila gave the signal. Seeing her, Janie froze. "What should I do?" she asked herself. She looked down, not wanting to meet Sheila's glance.

"If I take the blouse, will I get caught?" she wondered. Then she came back to the same question. "What should I do?"

TO TALK ABOUT

▶What do you think Janie did? Why do you think that?

▶Why did Janie want to be Sheila's friend? Why did she like being part of the group?

▶When someone is lonely or has poor self-esteem, it can be more tempting to do something wrong. Why?

▶How did Janie's thinking change after she entered the store?

▶If Janie stole the blouse and got away with it, what do you believe God would think about it? How would Janie feel about herself?

▶Some other time Janie's problem might be different. If Sheila wanted her to steal, what else might she pressure Janie to do?

▶Have you ever had an experience like this? If kids

pressure you to do something wrong, what should you do?

▶ Is friendship based on a wrong action ever a true friendship? How do you know?

▶ Are any of your friendships bad for you? What can you do about them?

When sinners tempt you, don't give in. (Proverbs 1:10, GNB)

Jesus, I want to be liked, and it's easy to go along with what other kids do. Show me how to say no so strongly that other kids don't bother me again. Give me Christian friends that want to live Your way.

BETTER THAN AN "A"

The bus had nearly reached Eric's farm when Marty asked him the question.

"Want to go to the game tonight? My brother said he'd give us a ride."

Eric couldn't think of anything he'd like better. Grantsburg, the small town where he went to school, had a good team this year. One more win and they'd go to district. "Sure," he said, "What time?"

Half an hour later Eric had a problem. "Sorry, but you can't go," Mom said. "You need to study."

"Aw, Mom!"

"Remember that letter about your grades? You have to do better in social studies. Last night you said you have a test tomorrow."

"I'll study right now. If I miss the game, I'll just sit and think about it. It won't do me any good to stay home."

"Sorry," answered Mom. "You've got chores first. Go call Marty."

Marty wasn't any help. "Aw, you don't need to study. I'm not going to. The test will just cover all the stuff we've been quizzed on."

Eric got off the phone feeling angry. "Dumb old social studies." Just the same, he knew he hadn't read even half the pages.

Later, as he opened his social studies book, Eric thought about all the kids piling into the school gym. Everyone from the whole area would be there. His friends would meet on the top bleacher.

As Eric stared out the window, the yard light broke the darkness. Yet in his mind he saw only the gym and Patrick O'Leary dribbling the ball across the court. Patrick was Grantsburg's top scorer.

"Maybe I'll be just as good a player someday," thought Eric. "I'm good now. In a few more years. . . ."

But if he didn't get his grades up, Mom and Dad wouldn't let him go out for basketball. He sighed.

Looking down at his book, he realized he had turned pages without remembering one thing he read.

Starting over, he did his best to concentrate. This time it began to make sense. Taking out his notebook,

Eric outlined the material the way his teacher had shown him.

Next he made a list of things he needed to memorize. On one side of the paper he wrote the states. Opposite them, he listed their capital cities. Then he folded the paper in half and tested himself.

By the time he went to bed, Eric felt good about what he'd learned. "Bet I'll cream that test," he thought. He couldn't remember ever studying so hard.

The following morning Eric didn't like hearing about the terrific game he'd missed. But his good feelings returned when he took the test. Never before had he been able to hurry through, sure of the answers. Only in a few places did he have trouble. On those he guessed and hoped for the best.

The next day the test came back with a large B at the top. "GREAT!" the teacher had written in bold letters. "BIG IMPROVEMENT!"

For the first time all year, Eric felt proud of his grade. "Wait 'til Mom and Dad see this," he thought.

"How did you do?" asked Marty from across the aisle.

"Got a B," said Eric, satisfaction in his voice. "I really studied. How about you?"

"Oh, what I usually get," answered Marty. Quietly he slid his test paper under a book, but before it disappeared, Eric saw his grade.

"A!" he thought. "Another A! I don't understand.

How does Marty always do it?"

Eric liked Marty. He liked the way he never made a big thing about getting better grades. Yet just then all Eric could think about was the game he missed.

"Marty went, and didn't study. I missed the game, and didn't get as good a grade," he thought. "It's not fair."

Somehow the B didn't seem important any more. In comparison with Marty's A, it didn't stack up.

"What's the use?" thought Eric. "My grades will never be as good as his. I could just as well have gone to the game."

Eric knew that wasn't really true, but the rest of the day it was all he thought about. "I don't know if I want to study that hard again," he told himself. He didn't know what he'd do the next time a test rolled around.

TO TALK ABOUT

▶What was Eric's long-term goal? How will it help him to think about that goal?

▶What are some possible reasons why Marty didn't need to study?

▶Which is more important for Eric, to compare his B with what he's done before, or to compare it with Marty's A? Why do you think this story is called "Better Than an 'A'"?

▶Do you compare your weaknesses with someone else's strengths? Why does that hurt your self-esteem?

▶What are some things you do well? How can those things help you become an in-spite-of-it kid?

Do your best to win full approval in God's sight, as a worker who is not ashamed of his work. (2 Timothy 2:15, GNB)

Thank You, Lord, that You can help me do my best, even in areas that are hard for me. Help me to not compare my weaknesses with someone else's strengths. Remind me of the things I do well.

SOMETHING TO OFFER

Spring sunlight warmed Becky's face as she leaned against the wall of the school. Yet the warmth of the sun was not in her heart.

She always dreaded this moment. Whenever the girls in her class played softball, Becky relived her fear of being chosen last.

As she watched, Anna and Kim took their places. "Why do they always get to be captains?" Becky asked herself. Of course she knew. They were the best players. Yet she felt upset over something that never seemed to change.

The choosing of sides began. "Stacey!" called out Anna.

"Judy!" shouted Kim.

And so it went. One moment Becky pressed hard against the wall, wishing she could disappear forever. The next she stood as tall as possible, hoping Anna or Kim would notice her. "If I could at least be somewhere in the middle," thought Becky. "I can't stand it if I'm last again."

But she was. When no one else was left, Anna called her name. Full of misery, Becky went forward, hating even the ground she had to cross.

"I'll show 'em," she thought. "I'll play so well that next time they'll *want* me on their team."

Straightening her shoulders, Becky walked quickly to her usual place in right field. For a long time nothing happened. Becky stood there, kicking blades of grass and squinting against the sun. Then a long, slow fly ball headed her way.

Becky ran forward. "If only I can. . . ." She reached up. The ball hit her thumb and dropped to the ground.

Grabbing wildly, Becky stumbled, and fell on the ball. As she scrambled up, two runners crossed home plate. Desperately she threw the ball to second. But even there she was too late. Just then the batter touched third.

"Way to go, butterfingers!" someone called.

Becky's face felt like it had caught fire. The rest of the afternoon it burned. When she returned to school the next morning, Becky still felt the flames of embarrassment.

She was glad when Mr. Lopez asked them to take out their math books. Becky flew through the problems. As she finished, she looked up. Everyone else was still working.

Across the aisle, Anna was doodling with a pencil. Today she didn't seem like a softball captain. One look told Becky that Anna was as confused as ever.

Secretly Becky felt glad. "Nice to know I can beat her at something."

But a moment later Anna looked her way. "Can you help me, Becky?" she whispered. "My head feels like it's spinning."

"Forget it!" thought Becky. "When you always choose me last? I should help *you*?"

An instant later she felt ashamed of her thoughts. Raising her hand, she got permission from Mr. Lopez, and slid her desk closer to Anna's.

"I just don't get it at all," said Anna in a low voice.

Step-by-slow-step, Becky started to explain. Each time she saw the confusion in Anna's face she moved back a step, then worked forward again.

At last a light seemed to turn on behind Anna's eyes. "Wow, Becky! How do you do it? You help me so much!"

In that moment Mr. Lopez asked for their attention. "I just received a note from the office about why Kim isn't in school today. It's really bad news. Her house caught fire last night. By the time the fire engine got there, the house had burned to the ground."

"Ohhh!" The gasp went through the room. Becky saw the shock in the faces around her.

"All of the family got out safely," said Mr. Lopez. "But they have nothing left but the clothes they were wearing."

Again Becky looked around the classroom. She wondered if her face looked as scared as those around her. "How awful!" she thought. "What if someone *hadn't* gotten out?"

Becky remembered how she had felt about Kim being one of the captains. Somehow being chosen last didn't matter anymore. Instead, Becky felt relieved that Kim was okay.

Her thoughts jumped ahead. "What would it be like to have nothing at all?"

"Let's think of what we can do to help Kim and her family," said Mr. Lopez.

For a minute everyone was quiet. All the feelings Becky had while playing softball rose to the surface. "What can I do?" she wondered. "It seems I can't do anything right."

Then Anna waved her hand. "I'll bring some of my clothes," she blurted out.

Paul chimed in. "I have little brothers about the age of Kim's brothers. I'll ask Mom for some of their things."

"We can bring cans of food," said Anna.

Becky was still thinking. Her mind seemed frozen by yesterday and how dumb she felt. "Is there really any way I can help?" she wondered.

As though hearing her question, Paul spoke again. "Maybe we should bring money."

"Good idea," said Mr. Lopez. "They'll have a lot of things to buy."

In that instant, a thought flashed through Becky's mind. "I can't play softball, but I sure know how to add money."

Her hand went up. "If you want, I'll be treasurer, and turn the money in to Mr. Lopez."

The teacher nodded, looking grateful.

Becky leaned back in her desk. For the first time since yesterday she felt warm inside, as though she had a place. She had something to offer.

TO TALK ABOUT

▶Becky made a choice to help both Anna and Kim. Why was that hard for her to do? What negative feelings did she have to forget?

▶Becky promised to collect the money. What do you think she will gain as she helps someone else? When you've helped others, how have you felt about yourself?

▶The next time the girls play softball Anna could choose Becky sooner, even though Becky doesn't play well. But how could Anna help Becky improve her game?

▶Are there skills you could improve if someone helped you? Why might it be important to grow in those skills, if possible?

▶When we can't succeed at something, we can *compensate*, or make up for it, by achieving in other ways. In what ways did Becky compensate for her clumsiness in softball? Can you think of ways you've compensated for skills you don't have?

Jesus said, "Give to others, and God will give to you. Indeed, you will receive a full measure, a generous helping, poured into your hands—all that you can hold. The measure you use for others is the one that God will use for you." (Luke 6:38, GNB)

Jesus, it bothers me when I can't do things I really want to do. If You want me to learn, give me someone who will help me. Or show me the things I can do well and help me grow in those areas. Thank You!

COREY GOES TO CAMP

"Hey, we're here!" said Corey. Poking Ross, he pointed to a sign outside the car window. "See? Spirit Point!"

For two months Corey had looked forward to church camp. Now the big moment was here!

Ross leaned across Corey. Sure enough, the arrow pointed off to the right. Minutes later, they climbed out of the car and said goodbye to Corey's dad. A counselor waited to show them where to go.

The cabin they entered was one large room with six bunk beds. Two other boys were already there. Suddenly Corey felt shy about meeting them. He was glad he'd been able to come with Ross. Ross would know what to say. As usual, he helped Corey out.

"Hi, I'm Ross. This is my friend Corey."

A tall boy with blonde hair popped up from where he was putting his clothes. "I'm Steve, and this is Jay. We're from Waite Park. How about you?"

Soon Ross had stowed his clothes, and he and Steve decided to check out the beach. Not sure what to do, Corey followed them and sat down on the dock to listen.

"Wish I could act like Ross," he thought. "He always thinks of something to talk about."

A moment later Ross and Steve headed for the canteen. There they found more kids.

Soon Steve introduced Ross to friends from Waite Park. Corey hung back, afraid to follow them. "I'll never think of something to say," he told himself.

By suppertime Corey felt lost and alone. When the bell rang for lights out, he crawled into bed, glad no one could see his face. A knot of misery formed in his stomach.

Burying his face in the pillow, Corey let his loneliness sink in. It was a long time before he fell asleep.

When he woke up the next morning, Corey discovered Ross and Steve had gone to the early-bird swim. "Now, what do I do?" he wondered.

Corey looked for Jay, but couldn't see him. The other guys were all getting dressed. Corey got up and pulled on his jeans, afraid that everyone would leave him behind.

114

Soon he was ready, but he pretended he had more to do. The loneliness he felt the night before was growing.

Just then Ross ran into the cabin. "Catch!" he called to Steve, throwing him a ball. Both boys laughed as though they had a private joke.

"I wish I could go home," thought Corey. "I'll never make it through a whole week."

Everyone in the cabin went to breakfast together, but Corey walked without talking, unable to think of anything to say. At breakfast Ross and Steve sat at one end of the table, still laughing over something that happened while swimming. Corey sat at the other end, staring at his French toast. For the first time in his life he wasn't hungry.

Just then the camp director rang a bell. "Small groups in ten minutes! Look at your name tag, and it will tell you where to go."

Corey glanced at his tag. Ross's had a different shape, so they'd be separated again. "I wonder if I can sneak back to the cabin and hide," thought Corey. But soon the kids were getting rid of their dirty dishes. Corey found Jay waiting for him.

"Looks like we're in the same group," he said. "Let's go together."

Minutes later they were part of a circle sitting on the grass outside the dining hall. "I'm Tim," said their leader. "And I know you're from many different churches. Let's start by each of you getting to know one other person. The easiest way is to ask questions. What are some questions you might ask?"

No one spoke. Tim sat there, waiting.

"What's the first thing you want to know about a person?" he asked.

"Their name," answered someone across the circle.

"Good. What else?"

"Where they live."

"Great!" said Tim. "Got any more ideas?"

No one spoke. "Then I've got some questions. Any of you have a giraffe at home?"

Everyone laughed.

"How about an elephant?"

Again they laughed.

"Well, what *do* you have at home?"

"A brother!" yelled someone, as though she didn't like the idea.

Someone else caught on. "A sister!"

"Gerbils!"

"Ahhhh!" said Tim. "Now, have you got something else you can ask a person besides their name?"

As Corey listened he made a discovery. "All I have to do is figure out what someone else wants to talk about," he thought.

Tim split them up two-by-two. Corey felt glad he could be with Jay. Now he knew what to say. "I know your name, but do you live in town or on a farm?"

It wasn't long before he discovered Jay had a pony named Samson, two sisters, and one brother. And he wanted to go fishing that afternoon.

"Maybe he's been feeling the way I have," thought Corey, glad he had a new friend.

Corey settled into a more comfortable position, surprised to discover he no longer felt lonely. The week ahead stretched out before him, filled with promise.

TO TALK ABOUT

▶How did Corey depend on Ross? Is it good to depend on someone that much? Why?

▶When Corey was lonely, who was he thinking about? How does focusing on ourselves keep us feeling lonely?

▶There was Someone Corey forgot. Who was that Person? How did He help Corey, even though Corey forgot about Him?

▶When did Corey's loneliness start to disappear? How did Corey become an in-spite-of-it kid?

▶If you want to choose between shyness and making a new friend, what are some questions to ask?

▶How do you think Corey felt about himself after he made friends with Jay? Why do you think that?

When you pass through the waters, I will be with you. (Isaiah 43:2)

Thank You, Jesus, that You have promised to be with me. Thank You that You're always my friend. When I'm lonely, help me remember that. Help me go beyond my shyness and reach out to others.

GRANDMA'S STORY

Kelly was staying with her grandparents for the weekend. She liked being with them. Grandma seemed to know how she felt about things, even when Kelly didn't tell her. Though Grandma was seventy-six, she still stood tall and straight and slender.

Grandpa was shorter than Grandma was and had rough, square hands from working as a carpenter. His eyes crinkled at the corners, and he always looked ready to laugh. He liked to tease Kelly.

"Come on, we're going out for a fish dinner," he said.

Kelly grinned. Grandpa knew she didn't like fish, and she knew Grandpa and Grandma didn't care

119

much for pizza. But they knew Kelly liked it. She felt like laughing as she guessed they had planned a special time for her.

Sure enough, Grandpa pulled up in front of the pizza place and let Kelly and Grandma out. As they waited on the sidewalk, some of Grandma's friends came by. Grandma introduced them, leaving a boy about Kelly's age until last. "This is their son Stephen," she said.

Kelly smiled her hello to everyone, and especially to Stephen. "He's about my age," she thought. "He looks nice."

But then Kelly knew her smile had frozen on her lips. She felt tall and awkward, as though she were bending over to talk with him. "I must be a whole head taller than he is," she told herself.

Suddenly every thought vanished from Kelly's head. She couldn't come up with one thing to say. When Stephen asked where she lived she could hardly answer.

Kelly was relieved when Grandpa came, and the three of them went into the restaurant. While Grandpa ordered pizza, Kelly and Grandma waited in a booth.

For Kelly the fun had gone out of the day. All she could think about was the feeling of looking down on Stephen. "I'm bigger than any kid my age," she thought with embarrassment. "I'd like to crawl in a hole and disappear forever."

120

Sliding down on the bench, she hoped no one would notice how tall she was, even when sitting.

Grandma broke into her thoughts. "Kelly, did I ever tell you how your grandfather and I met?"

Kelly shook her head, still remembering how short Stephen had been.

"When I was about twenty years old, I went to visit one of my cousins for the weekend. For Saturday night she invited a bunch of friends for a big treasure hunt."

"Where you have clues and go from place to place until you find the treasure?"

Grandma nodded. "My cousin divided us up as couples. She matched me with Andy, your grand-father. I was upset. There were two tall, good-looking boys in the group. I wanted to be with one of them."

Grandma laughed, remembering that long-ago time. Kelly knew the feeling, but she sure didn't feel like laughing about it.

"I thought I was big and awkward and at least a foot taller than Andy. I slumped my shoulders and hoped I could somehow look shorter."

Now Kelly felt uncomfortable. Once again Grandma had guessed her thoughts. Kelly slid up on the bench, took a deep breath, and straightened her shoulders.

"But Andy teased me," said Grandma. "He called me Skyscraper! I was hopping mad. I didn't want to go around the block with him, let alone on a treasure hunt."

Grandma smiled. "But the teams were all set. Your grandfather and I went from clue to clue, always just a minute or two ahead of everyone. When we came to the last clue, we were in the lead."

Kelly leaned forward, listening.

"The clue was tucked in a tin can in the hollow of a tree. When I shone the flashlight, I was tall enough to see the glint of the tin. Andy couldn't see it at all." Grandma paused.

"Go on," said Kelly.

"I thought, 'If I tell him I see it, he'll know it's because I'm taller. He'll tease me again.'"

"What happened?" asked Kelly.

"Just then I heard a noise. Another couple was close on our trail. I reached up, grabbed the can, took out one clue, and stuffed the can back in its place. We won the treasure!"

"What was it?" asked Kelly.

Grandma laughed. "A fake diamond ring, and two tickets to a play. Andy had to take me out again. He groaned and pretended that was no treasure. He got me to laugh about being taller than he was. It was the first time I'd ever laughed about being tall."

Kelly couldn't imagine laughing at something like that. "And you kept going together?"

A slow smile curved Grandma's lips. "I started to

realize it was probably even harder for him to be short than for me to be tall—especially if he liked me. Eventually we got married. I've never been sorry. I've always known how much I mean to Andy."

"It didn't matter? That you're taller, I mean?"

Grandma shook her head. "You come from a long line of tall people, Kelly. It's hard now, but many of the boys will catch up. A few will even pass you. If you slump your shoulders, you'll look tired, or discouraged, or ashamed of how you look."

Just then Grandpa set the pizza on the table. But Grandma kept talking, "If you stand up straight, you'll let people see how nice you are on the inside."

"And you'll get a good-looking husband like me," said Grandpa with a wink.

Kelly grinned. "I'll have to think about it," she said, reaching for the pizza. But to herself she added, "Maybe that wouldn't be so bad after all."

TO TALK ABOUT

▶All of us have something we don't like about the way we're made. We're too tall, too short, too fat, or too thin. Our nose is too long, or our ears too big. Sometimes there are things we can change about ourselves. Other times we need to accept the way we are. What are some things about yourself you'd like to change? What are some things you need to accept?

▶What happens to your self-esteem if you keep thinking about what you don't like about yourself?

▶Why are girls often taller than boys at this age?

▶If tall persons stand tall, what happens to their appearance? Does that give a clue about how to handle anything else you don't like about yourself? Give an example.

▶The Bible says that God saw you before you were born, even while you were being made. If you don't like the way you are, what are you telling God about how He made you?

▶What is something you *like* about the way you're made? How does it help your self-esteem to know the strengths God has given you?

▶Someone has said, "It's not how you look, but who you are that's important." How can you put that idea into practice?

My frame was not hidden from you when I was made in the secret place. (Psalm 139:15)

Father, You know that often I don't like the way I'm made. Yet because You created me this way, I choose to accept the way I am. I choose to develop the strengths You have given me. Thank You!

TELL ME MORE

For as long as Mark could remember, he had been good with a basketball. As he showered and dressed, he relived the game.

At the end of the first quarter, the Pirates were trailing. By the half they were still behind, with the gap narrowing. Then Mark hit a winning streak. As his teammates fed the ball to him, he dribbled in for layups. One ball after another went in. Whenever he couldn't break free, he tried for long shots. Even those swished through the net.

Now, with an easy grin on his face, Mark accepted the congratulations all around him. Yet as the locker room emptied out, he stayed behind. For some reason the victory seemed empty. Mark couldn't understand it. "I've worked a long time for this day," he thought, sitting down on a bench. "I've got everything going for me. But it doesn't seem like enough."

Elbows on his knees, he stared at the floor. "What's wrong with me? Why do I feel so empty inside?"

Just then Rusty came into the locker room. "Great game, Mark!"

Rusty was the equipment manager, and now he sat down beside Mark on the bench. "Hey, what's the matter?"

With anyone else Mark would have said, "Nothing! Bug off!" But he liked Rusty. At first when Mark met him, he seemed like a geek. The shortest boy in the class, Rusty's nickname came from his red hair and freckles. On the outside, he seemed exactly opposite from the hero Mark thought himself to be.

A couple of months earlier, Mark had started noticing Rusty. "No one pays any attention to him," he thought. "No one even thanks him. How come he seems to like what he's doing?"

Rusty always seemed to be carrying something— the basketballs, or whatever someone else forgot. Rusty did his job without saying much. Yet when the team needed help, he was always there.

Now, as Mark faced him, he wondered again. "How come you're student manager?" he asked.

"'Cause I like basketball."

"Why don't you play?"

"Well, I tried," said Rusty. "I used to dream about being a player like you. But I didn't make the team."

"That's a tough break," said Mark.

"Yeah," Rusty answered, his voice matter-of-fact. "I used to feel that way. But I sure wouldn't say that to someone like you."

"You don't feel bad anymore?"

Rusty laughed. "Nope, not anymore."

Mark was curious. "How come? I'd hate it if I couldn't play."

"Well, I'm not sure you'd understand," answered Rusty, his voice sounding as if he were feeling his way.

"Aw, sure I would," said Mark.

"Wellll," Rusty said again. "It has to do with how God made me."

"God talk!" thought Mark, ready to shut out words he didn't want to hear, the way he always did. He stood up to go, then remembered the empty space inside.

Rusty kept talking. "God could have made me just like you," he said. "It would have been great if He had. But He didn't. This is the way God made me."

Rusty stood up, spread his arms wide, and grinned. "This is me—all there is!"

Mark laughed at him. "I've never met anyone like you, Rusty!"

At the same time he was curious. Mark knew all

129

the advantages of being what he was. The tallest boy in the class. The best basketball player. "How can someone like Rusty make a joke of what he isn't?" he wondered. Yet he was afraid to ask.

Rusty looked at Mark's face and guessed. "Sounds dumb, huh? You think I'm just pretending to like the way I am?"

Mark knew enough to be embarrassed. "Well, now that you mention it."

This time Rusty spoke with a sureness in his voice that startled Mark. "I feel good about who I am because I know how much God loves me."

Mark swore. "That's a bunch of ____"

But Rusty was unshaken. "No, it's not."

Mark picked up his gym bag and started for the door. Halfway there, he stopped and turned. The emptiness inside seemed to demand an answer. "Hey, how do you know God loves you? What makes you think that?"

Rusty spoke quickly, as though he knew he wouldn't have another chance. "Because Jesus died for me. He loves me so much that He died on a cross. He loves you too, Mark, the same way."

For a long moment Mark stood there, feeling embarrassed. He couldn't decide whether to keep on going or turn around. Finally he set down his gym bag and came back.

"Tell me more, Rusty," he said.

TO TALK ABOUT

▶If Rusty *didn't* like the way God created him, why would he find it hard to reach out to Mark?

▶Who gave Rusty the power to talk with Mark, even though Mark laughed at what he said?

▶God uses other people to help us feel loved and good about ourselves. He also gives us an important reason for self-esteem. Why did Rusty feel good about who he is?

▶What's the difference between feeling good about ourselves and being conceited? How can we keep from getting conceited?

▶You may be the only person who's able to talk with the kids who surround you each day. Do some of them need to know Jesus? How can you pray for them? How can you talk with them?

▶Maybe you're like Mark and feel an empty space inside. If you're wondering what it means to know Jesus as your Savior and Lord, think about these steps:

> 1) *Jesus loves you.* "For God loved the world so much that he gave his only Son, so that everyone who believes in him may not die but have eternal life." (John 3:16, GNB)
>
> 2) *Jesus died for your sin.* "God has shown us how much he loves us—it was while we were still

sinners that Christ died for us!" (Romans 5:8, GNB)

3) *Tell Jesus you're sorry for your sin. Ask for-giveness.* "If we say we have no sin, we deceive ourselves, and there is no truth in us. But if we confess our sins to God, he will keep his promise and do what is right: he will forgive us our sins and purify us from all our wrongdoing." (1 John 1:8-9, GNB)

4) *Ask Jesus to be your Savior and Lord.* "Everyone who calls upon the name of the Lord will be saved." (Romans 10:13)

If you'd like to invite Jesus into your life, you can pray these words:

Thank You, Jesus, that You love me. Thank You for dying for me. I'm sorry for my sin, and I ask You to forgive me. I ask You to be my Savior and Lord. Thank You for my salvation, and that it begins right now!

BUGS BUNNY KLUMPERS

Kevin's brothers and sisters surrounded him in the family room. It was his oldest brother, Pete, who started it all. Looking at Kevin's shoes, he started laughing. "Hey, Klumpers! You've got Bugs Bunny feet!"

Then his sister pointed to Kevin's long fingers. "Wow, Kev! You not only have big feet. Your hands are GIGANTIC!"

That did it. Kevin swallowed hard, pretending he didn't care. But he wished he could sneak away. He felt miserable inside.

"Oh, shut up!" he said, wanting to strike back in any way he could. "You're not so great-looking yourself!"

Yet he wondered, "Why do kids always pick on me? I must be as lousy as they think." At home, school, or church, it was always the same. Kids took every chance they got to torment him.

Finally Mom called a halt to the teasing. "Don't listen to them, Kevin," she said. "Pretty soon you'll have a growth spurt. The rest of your body will catch up with your hands and feet."

But her words didn't comfort Kevin. One picture stayed in his mind—Bugs Bunny's huge feet.

That evening Kevin was still thinking about this new name. Even worse, he could remember every other name kids had called him. It didn't matter how long ago—he could remember. In his mind he piled those names one on top of another. Not even Bugs Bunny could jump over the mountain they made.

Standing in front of the mirror in his bedroom, Kevin stared at himself. "It's not just my hands and feet. My nose is too big too," he thought.

Standing there, he glanced at a picture of Pete tucked between the frame of the mirror and the glass. The picture showed Pete ready to ride off on his bike. Taken at least three years before, Pete was about the age Kevin was now.

Looking at it more closely, Kevin felt surprised. "His feet were just as big as mine! And his hands look like great big bear paws! How come it didn't bug him?"

Dropping down on his bed, Kevin lay there, staring up at the ceiling. It took a lot of thought, but at last he felt a camera flash go off in his mind. As though a picture had been snapped and the moment kept forever, Kevin remembered a scene a few years ago.

A neighborhood kid named Rob had spied Pete's lawn-mowing shoes. Stretched out of shape, they looked even bigger than the usual klumpers Pete wore.

Rob roared with laughter. "What big feet you have!" he said, as though he were Little Red Riding Hood meeting the wolf.

"The better to kick you with!" Pete flipped back. They both laughed.

Thinking about it now, Kevin couldn't remember another time Rob teased Pete about his feet.

"I bet kids bug me because they know I can't take it," thought Kevin.

In the days that followed, he worked hard at trying something new. At first it felt strange. He had a hard time coming up with funny answers instead of hurt feelings. Sometimes the moment was over before he figured out what to say. But when Pete called out, "Hey, Klumpers! You with the big feet!"

Kevin answered, "Yep. The better to kick you with!"

Pete looked at him and grinned. Then suddenly, as though he saw something new in Kevin, Pete slapped him on the back.

From that time on, the name was a game between them, instead of something that hurt. And because he felt Pete understood, Kevin felt great way down to the end of his Bugs Bunny toes.

TO TALK ABOUT

▶What choice did Kevin make about how he wanted to handle kids who teased him? How did he become an in-spite-of-it kid?

▶What's the difference between knocking yourself and laughing at yourself? Give examples from Kevin's story.

▶What's the difference between having kids laugh *at* you and laugh *with* you?

▶Sometimes kids tease because they know someone like Kevin can't take a joke. Other times they tease because they know the person *can* take it and respond in the right way. How can you know if a kid is being mean in teasing you? How can you know if kids tease because they like and respect you? How does knowing that difference affect your self-esteem?

▶Kevin reacted to teasing by teasing back. Yet if someone always reacts by trying to be a clown, that person may be covering up hurt. What are some ways Kevin could tell his family that he doesn't want to be teased about his feet anymore?

▶If you like to tease others, how can you know when

they have had enough and it's time to stop?
▶Are there some things we shouldn't tease about?
What are they? How can that kind of teasing
seriously hurt a person?

---

*He [God] will yet fill your mouth with laughter and
your lips with shouts of joy.* (Job 8:21)

*Jesus, when kids tease me I keep thinking about
what they say and I feel terrible. Show me how to
handle teasing. Help me so I don't take myself too
seriously. If I need to, help me to even laugh at
myself.*

FROM THE PITCHER'S MOUND

Amber plopped down on the bench, rested her chin on her hands, and stared at the ground. "What's happening to me anyway?" she asked herself.

Only last week she had pitched a no-hit game for her team, the Cardinals. Each time she threw the ball it went exactly where she wanted. When they won, the coach and team hugged her, shouting, "Great game, Amber!"

But today—wow! What a difference. First she'd let a player walk. Next she fumbled a fly. Finally the other team batted a home run, bringing in three players and ending the game.

Now Amber felt dusty and tired. A shower would

help, but it wouldn't wash off the feeling that she'd let her team down. That would probably never leave.

Taking a deep breath, she started toward the parking lot. "Days like this I hate myself. What's wrong with me?"

Partway to the car, Amber stopped and waited for her family to catch up. Just then she heard someone talking on the other side of a van.

"She's too sure of herself," said the voice. "She's letting her game slide."

A low mumble answered, and Amber couldn't pick out the words. Then the first voice spoke again. "If Coach had let me in, I would have turned it around. I'm a better pitcher any day."

"Polly!" thought Amber. "My old friend Polly. Or my used-to-be friend. Used-to-be before she wanted to be a pitcher."

Amber's anger churned. "If that's my friend, I don't need an enemy!"

She felt like stomping around to the other side of the van. "I'd like to walk right up to Polly and tell her what I think. I'd make her take back every word!"

Losing the game was bad enough. Now this— Amber felt completely wiped out.

A moment later Amber's parents caught up with her. "You tried your hardest," said Mom, giving her a squeeze. Usually she and Dad could cheer Amber up, but it didn't seem to help today. Amber felt like a softball splitting apart at the seams.

The next afternoon Amber discovered the game wasn't over. She saw kids look at her, then glance away without meeting her eyes. Once she heard a whisper, "Taking her game for granted."

Suddenly she knew. Polly had started a whispering campaign.

An anger unlike any Amber had ever known shot through her. Whenever she thought of Polly, the sparks fanned into flames. Her feelings added fuel to the fire.

That anger still blazed when Amber took the pitcher's mound the next week. As she faced the first batter, Amber bit her lip and tried to stay calm. Yet it wasn't long until the ump shouted, "Ball four!"

The second batter got off a long hit between second and third. The crowd groaned. Amber knew she was losing her grip.

Taking a deep breath, she tried again. The wind-up. The pitch. Ohhh—a home run! The roar from the crowd sounded deafening to Amber.

"See? You're no good," it shouted.

She wasn't surprised when Coach called her out. Nor was she surprised to see Polly take her place. But Amber's anger leapt into a forest fire.

Sitting on the bench, elbows on her knees, Amber stared straight ahead. As the Cardinals fell further behind the Blue Jays, she watched every move of the game. Yet her thoughts churned round and round.

She felt desperate. For a long time Amber hadn't prayed, but she began now. Even so, her prayers didn't seem to get off the ground. Something seemed in the way between her and God.

The second inning passed. Then the third. Amber still sat on the bench. By the beginning of the fourth,

she started sorting out her choices. One word dropped into her mind.

"Forgive? You gotta be kidding, God. Polly was the one who started it."

Through the first half of that inning, Amber argued with herself and with God. "See? I *am* a better pitcher. Polly's losing the game. They're three runs ahead of us. We might never catch up!"

But the word stayed in her mind. "Forgive? I don't want to forgive."

One minute Amber felt ashamed of herself. The next she decided she didn't want to change the way she felt. "If I stop being mad, it will seem like Polly won."

Out on the field the game wasn't going well. The Blue Jays were four runs ahead with bases loaded. Until last week the Cardinals hadn't lost a game all season.

Then a thought struck Amber. "Here I sit, wanting Polly to lose so I look better. I'm almost rooting for the other team!"

Forgive? Suddenly Amber knew what choice to make. Eyes wide open, she stared ahead, praying silently. She used only four words. "Jesus, I forgive her."

In the next moment Amber felt the weight she'd carried all week drop off of her. "Yaaaaay!" she called out the next time she could. But it was more than a cheer for the Cardinals.

At the top of the fifth the Blue Jays came to bat. "Amber!" called the coach. "Go on in."

This time the ball felt sweet in Amber's hands. Thoughts of Polly were gone. Thoughts of how good she herself might look fell away. Even the crowd didn't seem important.

Glove high above her head, Amber snagged the ball, then caught the catcher's signal. "I'll do my best," she thought. "But I just want to play ball."

Facing the batter, she wound up. "It's just a game," she told herself. "Just a game."

The ball looked great going across the plate.

TO TALK ABOUT

▶What did Amber mean when she decided, "I just want to play ball"? What had changed in her thinking?

▶If you want to feel good about yourself, you have to forgive those who hurt you. Amber made that choice. She used her will to forgive Polly. What words did she pray?

▶When Amber forgave Polly, she felt she no longer carried a heavy weight. Yet you may forgive someone and not "feel" any different. Does your prayer of forgiveness still count? How do you know?

▶When someone hurts you, it may be important to talk with that person about it. Do you think Amber should talk with Polly about the things Polly said? Why or why not?

▶Whether Amber's team won or lost, Amber won something. What was it?

Jesus said, "If you forgive anyone his sins, they are forgiven; if you do not forgive them, they are not forgiven." (John 20:23)

Jesus, when someone hurts me, I want to hate that person. Yet even on the cross You prayed, "Father, forgive them." And so, Jesus, because of Your example I forgive the person who hurt me. Take away my bitter and angry feelings. Thank You!

145

HOW'S MY MOM?

They stood at the church door, ready to leave. Cheri looked at her mom, as if for the first time.

"She's really pretty!" Cheri thought. Mom's dark brown eyes sparkled and her lips curved in a smile.

As Mom shook hands with Pastor Evenson, he asked, "How are you doing?"

Mom smiled again. "Fine, just fine," she said.

Yet as Mom and Cheri and two-year-old Rachel walked the short distance home, Cheri noticed the shadow in Mom's eyes. Since Dad stopped living with them, Cheri had seen that shadow of unhappiness often. She dreaded what it meant, and hoped she was wrong.

As they ate lunch, Mom said, "Let's go for a bike ride." Soon they were off, Cheri on her own bike, and little Rachel in the bike seat behind Mom. The September day was perfect, and Mom seemed okay.

Once she stopped to point out the ducks on a pond. Another time she pulled up the hood on Rachel's sweatshirt to protect her from the wind. Mom had even brought treats along. After awhile they sat down by a lake to eat them.

But when they got home that evening, Mom started drinking again. As she downed one glass after another, Cheri blamed herself. "I thought I poured it all out," she groaned silently.

She pretended she didn't see what was happening. Yet as she watched TV she kept count, and her uneasiness grew. Sometimes when Mom drank she just got sad and talked strange. Other times she acted mean.

"Which way is Mom going to act?" Cheri wondered, feeling scared.

Soon she found out. In her funny toddler way Rachel went over to Mom and held up her bottle. Mom pushed the bottle aside.

Rachel tried again.

"Don't bother me!" snapped Mom, shoving the little girl away.

Rachel yowled. Cheri jumped up, and pulled her into the kitchen. After filling her bottle, she took

Rachel to the bedroom, changed her clothes, and put her to bed.

Feeling as though a giant hand twisted her insides, Cheri crept into her own bed. For a long time she lay there, afraid to fall asleep. She thought about the last time Mom got like this.

Though the night wasn't cold, Cheri started to shiver, remembering. Mom had come into the room, pulled her out of bed, and hit her. Now Cheri wondered, as she had a hundred times, "What did I do wrong?"

"Where are you, God?" she asked. "I'm so scared."

She thought about Sunday school that morning, and the verse the class had learned. Jesus told His disciples, "Let not your heart be troubled. You are trusting God, now trust in me" (John 14:1, TLB).

Cheri started to cry and covered her head with the blankets. Afraid Mom would hear, she buried her face in the pillow. "Let not your heart be troubled," she said to herself. "Let not your heart be troubled."

After a long time Cheri stopped sobbing, but her heart still cried out. "What should I do, Jesus? What should I do?"

As she finally faded off into sleep, Cheri wondered if she should tell someone. Just as quickly as the thought came to her mind, she tossed it out. "I don't want anyone to know how Mom acts," she thought, filled with shame. "I'd be embarrassed to tell them.

Besides, maybe it's all my fault."

The next morning Mom seemed better. She had the day off, but Cheri had school. "What about Rachel?" she wondered. "If I go, will she be okay? If I ask about it, Mom might get mad."

When she could wait no longer, Cheri finally left for school. Off and on through the day, she thought about Rachel. The minute school was out, Cheri hurried home.

As she walked up the front sidewalk, she heard Rachel crying and broke into a run. The little girl sounded as if she'd cried for a long time.

Bounding up the porch steps, Cheri tried to open the front door. It was locked. From somewhere Rachel still cried. Cheri's heart tugged at the sound.

She rattled the door, her feeling of panic growing. Then she ran along the porch to the front window. Peering in, Cheri saw Mom sprawled on the sofa, sound asleep. A bottle lay on the floor beside her.

Cheri felt sick. With another bound she was down the steps, heading around the side of the house. Once again she heard Rachel. Her crying seemed closer.

Following the sound, Cheri came to the backyard. There in full sunlight was Rachel's playpen.

As Rachel saw Cheri, she held up her arms and whimpered. Cheri picked her up and hugged her. As she looked at Rachel's sunburned arms and face, she broke into sobs.

"It's all my fault! If I hadn't gone to school. . . ."

Sitting down in the shade, Cheri cried as she had never cried before. Rachel nestled close in her arms. Through her tears Cheri looked down at her. "Oh, God, what should I do?" she asked. This time her cry for help was a prayer.

Two words dropped into her mind: "Tell someone." But Cheri still pushed the idea aside.

Then Rachel stirred in her arms. Gently Cheri touched the little girl's skin. It felt hot and dry with sunburn. Her eyelids and cheeks were puffy from crying. Once again Cheri's heart tugged.

Then she remembered Pastor Evenson looking at Mom and asking, "How are you doing?"

"Could I talk to him?" she wondered.

Staggering under Rachel's weight, Cheri stood up and started walking to church.

TO TALK ABOUT

▶What does it mean to say that someone has a drinking problem?

▶How did Cheri's mom change when she started drinking? Why was Cheri afraid of what her mom would do?

▶Her mom's drinking had affected Cheri's self-esteem. What are some clues that tell you how Cheri felt about herself?

▶When Cheri found Rachel sunburned and crying, she said, "It's all my fault." She asked, "What did I do wrong?" Was it Cheri's fault? Why or why not?

▶Cheri became an in-spite-of-it kid. She made a good choice in going to talk with Pastor Evenson. What do you think he'll do to help Cheri's mom?

▶If you or one of your friends need help because of a problem like Cheri's, there are people you can talk to. Who are they? Think of a school or Sunday school teacher, a pastor, neighbor, relative, or friend. There are also groups called Alcoholics Anonymous that help people who have a problem because of drinking.

▶Why does Jesus understand when we hurt because of hard things in our lives? If we ask Him to heal us, how can He help us feel better?

Whoever goes to the Lord for safety, whoever remains under the protection of the Almighty, can say to him, "You are my defender and protector. You are my God; in you I trust." (Psalm 91:1-2, GNB)

Thank you, God, for caring about what happens to me. If I'm ever in trouble, give me someone to help me. Protect me. Take away my scared feelings and heal me. Thanks for being my big God!

I'M DIFFERENT

"I want to go," said David.

"I *don't* want you to go," answered Dad.

David looked around the supper table, wondering if he could get help from his older brother, Scott, or younger sister, Tina. Right now neither of them looked ready to come to his rescue.

"David, why do you want to go to this video party?" asked Mom.

"'Cause it'll be fun," he answered. "It's fun to be with the other kids."

"That's a good reason," said Dad. "But the last time you went to Tom's house you saw a video we didn't want you to see. This one's no better."

"Aw, Dad, all my friends are gonna see it. If I don't,

153

I won't know what to talk about at school."

"You'll feel out of it," said Mom.

David turned to her, surprised that Mom seemed to be on his side. "Right! All the other parents are letting their kids go. If I don't see the video, I'll be different from everyone else."

"Hummm," said Dad. "I wonder if our family is different in other ways?"

"Yeah," said Tina. "I'm different. I don't get to stay up as late as my friends."

"Maybe we should all think about it," said Mom. "Let's see what we come up with by supper tomorrow night."

When David went to school the next morning, he looked for ways his family was different. "Maybe I can still talk Dad into letting me go to the party," he thought.

Instead he started thinking about one kid after another and how they looked. In math he saw all different colors of hair and skin. Some kids were tall and others short. Some were fat and others thin.

In gym class he noticed differences in ability. As the kids played volleyball, some of them always seemed to hit the ball into the air or smash it over the net. Other kids never did.

At the end of the day he stood at his locker, ready to go home. Around him, kids called to each other. "See ya, J.J.!" Or "Hey, Frog, coming over to my house tonight?" Almost everyone had a different name.

But late that afternoon when Mom called him in for supper, David thought of a way his family was different. It would take him longer than other kids to get back out to play. His family always talked about what had happened that day.

David decided to put that time to good use. "Maybe I've got enough ammunition to change Dad's mind," he thought, digging into the fried chicken.

Partway through the meal, Dad asked, "Well, what did you come up with? What are some ways our family is different?"

David started off. "When the parents of other kids drive us somewhere, they almost always play rock music. You listen to a Christian station or classical junk. Kids think I have a nutty family."

Tina chimed in. "I'm different 'cause we go to church and lots of kids don't."

"Atta girl," thought David. "I'm gonna get my way yet."

"I'm different because lots of my friends are good in sports," said Scott. "But I'm better in music."

Mom stood up and brought more hot rolls to the table. "I'm different because I turn down promotions instead of taking a job where I'd have to travel. If I took the promotions, I couldn't work when you kids are in school, and be home when you're home."

"Oh oh," thought David, feeling uneasy. "Maybe

155

this isn't gonna fly after all."

Dad pushed back his chair. "I'm different because I choose to be honest in business. A lot of people don't."

Suddenly David realized he wasn't going to get his way. In his disappointment he wanted to lash out and hurt Dad. "I'm different because this family wants to gab, and gab, and gab," he said. "Other kids get back out right after supper. They can do whatever they want."

But somehow his words didn't sound as mad as they could have. As David spoke, he suddenly realized he really did like the times the family shared around the table.

"That's right. We *are* different," said Dad. "But isn't there at least one way every person on earth is different from everyone else?"

David didn't want to answer Dad's question. He didn't want to meet his eyes. He just wanted to escape outside. Another question had dropped into David's mind. Maybe if he got away from the table he could push it aside. He sure didn't want to tell anyone what he was wondering. After all, what would other kids think?

But in the days that followed, David's question didn't go away. Every now and then it came back, and he started wondering again. "Is it sometimes *good* to be different?"

TO TALK ABOUT

▶Some kids *act* different and do stupid things because they want attention and don't know how to get it. How have you seen this happen?

▶Other times kids *feel* different because they refuse to do something that would hurt them. Have you needed to make that choice? What happened?

▶David felt different because his parents expected him to make good choices. How would it hurt David if his mom or dad never cared about the choices he made? Why?

▶When we worry about feeling different for *good* reasons, we're usually afraid of what people think. In what ways are you afraid of what other kids think? How does it affect what you do?

▶How would you answer David's question, "Is it sometimes good to be different?" How can feeling different from other kids sometimes protect you?

▶How was Jesus different from any other person who ever lived?

God says, "I, even I, am he who comforts you. Who are you that you fear mortal men, the sons of men, who are but grass, that you forget the LORD your Maker?" (Isaiah 51:12-13)

Jesus, I'm afraid of being different. I'm afraid of what other kids think. Help me believe it's Your approval that's important. Help me when I need to be different.

MORE THAN HOT LUNCH

J oy pushed her books into her locker and took off down the hall. Maybe she could manage to escape the kids if she left by a different door than usual.

But Nick must have been watching for her. As Joy tried to edge past a group of boys, he separated himself from the others and fell into step with her.

"Joy, I'm sorry about what happened at lunch today," he said.

Joy remained silent.

"I'm sorry about what the other guys said."

Still Joy didn't speak, and Nick began looking uncomfortable.

"Hey, Joy, help me out. I'm apologizing."

"I accept your apology," she said, her voice soft, but edged with hurt. "I forgive you."

"Then what's wrong? Forgive and forget, you know?"

Joy kept walking, gazing straight ahead. "I said I'd forgive you. I'll do my best to forget, but. . . ."

"But what?"

Joy looked straight into Nick's eyes. "Where were you when I needed you?"

Nick's face flushed red. "You wanted me to speak up," he muttered.

"Yes, I wanted you to speak up." Suddenly Joy's mouth trembled, as though she were going to cry. Once again she looked straight ahead, walking faster.

"We talked about this," she said. "Remember? We made an agreement. Sunday night at church we both said we wanted to witness more at school."

She looked at Nick, and he nodded.

"So today I wore this little cross and heart pin on my collar. I knew kids would ask what it means. They always do. I prayed it would give me a chance to talk about Jesus. It did. I was having a good talk with Lisa, until. . . ."

Nick finished for her. "Until Cody came past with a tray, heard what you were talking about, and brought the guys over."

"And you didn't back me up, or even seem to agree with me. You didn't say one word!"

Now it was Nick's turn to look straight ahead. "Joy. . . ."

Once again her voice was quiet, but there was a tone in it Nick had never heard before. "I've forgiven you, Nick. But where's the commitment you've been talking about? Did you mean what you said?"

Without another word, Joy turned and half-walked, half-ran the three blocks home. All she wanted was to reach her own room. As she shut the door, she tried to close out the day's events—the voices teasing her, calling her a Jesus freak. The laughter over what she'd said to Lisa. Nick's quiet eyes, just watching, saying nothing.

Joy's face burned hot thinking about how embarrassed she'd been. She wanted to cry. She wanted to be mad. She wanted to throw something. But most of all, she just hurt, way down inside.

Then she remembered Lisa. "She was listening, Lord. Lisa was listening until the boys started causing trouble. Will everything we talked about be wasted?"

Joy's shoulders started to shake, and the sobs came from the deepest part of her being. Picking up her Bible, she hugged it to her, as though she didn't know what else to do.

At last Joy opened it and turned to words she had memorized, but needed to read: "I assure you that whoever declares publicly that he belongs to me, the Son of Man will do the same for him before the angels of God. But whoever rejects me publicly, the Son of Man will also reject him before the angels of God" (Luke 12:8-9, GNB).

For a long time Joy stared at the words. Then she repeated them to herself. Finally she drew a long ragged breath, stood up, and gazed out the window. Her lips curved slightly, as though a smile were beginning.

TO TALK ABOUT

▶How do you feel about the way Nick acted when the boys started making fun of Joy?

▶What probably hurt Joy's self-esteem more—the teasing from the kids or Nick's failure to speak up?

▶Joy belongs to the in-spite-of-it club. Near the end of the story she seemed to receive comfort. What clues tell you that even though she was hurt, she became stronger because of what happened?

▶How do you think Jesus feels about Joy's efforts to witness? Or about Nick's failure to speak up? Why does Nick need to ask Jesus for forgiveness?

▶Why is it important that we try to witness, even though we're afraid?

▶Are there people Jesus wants you to witness to? Who are they? How can the Holy Spirit help you tell about Jesus, even when it's hard to witness? (For clues see Luke 12:11-12.)

Even if you should suffer for what is right, you are blessed. (1 Peter 3:14)

Jesus, I'm afraid of what other kids say. Yet I ask You to give me the Holy Spirit's power to tell others about You. If kids tease me, remind me how much You love me, and how much You want them to know Your love.

HE'S MY BROTHER

They had finished buying clothes for Darrin when Mom asked the question. "Mike, will you and Darrin go see the rock exhibit while I do my own shopping? It's in the other part of the mall."

Mike knew he couldn't say no. Long ago he'd learned that Mom needed help with Darrin. Yet that didn't mean he *wanted* to do what she asked.

Grasping the handgrips, he swung Darrin's wheelchair around. Carefully he steered through the narrow aisles between clothing displays. But his old question was back. "What if someone from school sees me?"

Three years older than Mike, Darrin had always

gone to a different school—one for kids with special needs. Darrin had been born with cerebral palsy [sehr-ee-bruhl pall-zee]. Because of the damage to his brain at birth or before, he often couldn't make his muscles do what he wanted.

As he looked down, Mike saw Darrin's arm jerk out. He knew his brother couldn't help it, any more than Darrin could help being in a wheelchair. But his arm caught a pile of shirts on a nearby counter, dragging several of them onto the floor.

Inwardly Mike groaned. "Why do we always have to attract attention?" Edging around the wheelchair, he started to pick up the shirts.

Off to the right a salesclerk turned. "What are you doing?" she asked.

As Mike knelt down, the clerk came closer and saw Darrin. "Oh, excuse me," she mumbled.

Darrin started to speak. Mike knew Darrin was trying to say he was sorry, but the clerk didn't wait to listen. Looking embarrassed by Darrin's stumbling sounds, she gathered up an armload of shirts, dropped them on the counter, and hurried off.

Mike turned in time to see the hurt in Darrin's eyes. Forcing himself to make the effort, he spoke. "It's okay, Darrin."

Darrin's mouth shaped a crooked smile. His words stumbled out. "Should I try it again?"

In spite of himself, Mike grinned. He also felt a bit

ashamed. For the first time he wondered, "What if I was the one in the wheelchair?"

Soon they came to the rock and mineral show. A crowd had gathered, but Mike did his best to get Darrin up where he could see. For as long as Mike could remember, Darrin had collected rocks. By now he owned over 200 and knew the scientific name of each one.

Darrin wanted to get closer to the geodes [jee-odes]. Gray on the outside and shaped like a ball, they had been cut open so people could see the colorful hollow at the center. Each hollow was lined with beautiful crystals.

Mike edged the wheelchair up to the table. The boy standing next to Darrin looked down and moved slightly, giving him more room.

Mike froze. "Brad!" he thought. "The best football player in school!"

Quietly Mike moved away from Darrin, thinking, "I hope Brad doesn't see me." Brad didn't. Soon he was talking with Darrin. Both of them had noticed the same rock.

"Geode," said Darrin, the word coming clearer than usual.

As he reached for the rock, his hand swung wild and missed. He tried again. This time, as his hand came back, he picked up the geode. With an effort he turned it so Brad could see the crystals.

Mike couldn't hear what Brad said. But as he watched, Brad leaned down, listening carefully. A moment later he grinned and nodded his head.

Just then Brad looked up and saw Mike. He motioned for him to come over. "Come here. I want to show you something," he said. "It's just the rock I need for my collection."

"You collect rocks?" asked Mike.

"Yeah," answered Brad. "But I don't have very many." He nodded toward Darrin. "He says he has 200. Mike, this is Darrin."

For a moment Mike argued with himself. "I could pretend I'm not with him. I could get away with it." Then he tossed out the idea.

"I know him," he answered. "He's my brother."

Darrin's head jerked in his direction, and then Mike knew. Darrin had caught something different in his voice.

Brad's eyes showed surprise. "Your brother?"

Deep inside, Mike realized that for the first time he'd accepted his brother just the way he was. "Yep," he said. "He's my brother."

TO TALK ABOUT

▶Cerebral palsy makes it hard for people to make their muscles do what they want. How would cerebral palsy affect Darrin's ability to walk, speak, pick up rocks, and other things?

▶How do you think Darrin felt about not being able to do the things he'd like?

▶Why was Mike embarrassed about his brother's disability?

▶As a football player, Brad gave Darrin some very special gifts. What were they?

▶Why was it important to Darrin's self-esteem that Mike chose to accept him just the way he was?

▶What happened to Mike's feelings when he told Brad, "He's my brother"? Why was it important to Mike's self-esteem that he accepted Darrin as he was?

▶Cerebral palsy affects people in a variety of ways, depending on the amount of brain damage. Some people are very limited in their physical activities. Others are not. Do you know anyone who has cerebral palsy or another kind of disability? How does it limit them? How can you help them?

Jesus said, "In everything, do to others what you would have them do to you." (Matthew 7:12)

Jesus, often I don't know how to act around people who can't do all the things I can. Help me accept them the way they are so I'm free to love them and myself.

171

A PHONE OF MY OWN

It all started in school that day. Marli's friend Karen had just gotten her own phone and private number. And Debbie came to school with a great new jacket—the kind Marli always wanted.

Listening to her friends talk, she wondered, "Why can't I have the things they have?"

All afternoon Marli thought about it. By the time she left for home, she'd convinced herself. "I'll start with the phone. Maybe if I bug Mom enough, she'll give in."

Mom was in the kitchen fixing supper when Marli opened the door. At Mom's feet, two-year-old Sunny played on the floor. Around Sunny lay all the pots and pans she had taken from the cupboard. Mom gave Marli a hug. "Have a good day?"

Marli nodded as though she really hadn't heard Mom's question.

At the kitchen table her little brother, Jesse, was coloring a picture. Proudly he held it up for Marli to see, but she barely noticed. Instead, she launched her attack.

"Karen's dad gave her a phone of her own."

Mom pushed the hair out of her eyes. "Marli, we've talked about this before."

"But I want to talk about it again. She has the phone in her room and her own private number."

"Karen's dad gets business calls at home," answered Mom. "He can't afford to have her tie up the phone."

"But if I had one, I could talk as long as I wanted."

Instead of answering, Mom started to peel the potatoes.

"I could talk without everyone listening," Marli added.

As she watched, Mom's shoulders sagged slightly. "I'm getting through," she thought. "I'll wear her down."

But in that moment Mom turned from the sink. "Even if we had the money, it wouldn't be good for you."

"Why not?" Marli asked.

Mom sighed, and the tired lines around her eyes seemed deeper. "Marli, have you heard yourself talk lately? 'I want, I want, I want.'"

"Yes, I want this," answered Marli, her voice filled with resentment. "If you wanted to give it to me, you could. You just don't love me enough."

"I love you so much I don't want you to be selfish," said Mom, her voice firm. "You need to know how to share the phone with the rest of us."

"Aw, Mom."

"The answer is no."

Marli ran to her room and didn't come out until supper. Except for saying "hi" to Dad, she was silent, the anger churning within her. Even when Sunny threw her plate on the floor, Marli sat unmoved, her face stony.

Cleaning up the mess, Mom looked like she was going to cry. But Marli pretended she didn't see.

Later that evening Marli plopped down in front of the TV. Dad was watching a special on public television.

"Who is she?" asked Marli.

"Mother Teresa," answered Dad. "A woman who's given her life helping the poor and dying in India."

Marli groaned. "Can't we watch something else?"

"I want to see this," said Dad. "Your turn next—if there's something good."

Marli waited, hoping the program would be over soon. On the screen a young woman spoke, describing

Mother Teresa. "Mother said she wanted to die on her feet. I think that's just what she's doing—giving herself to the last drop."

"Stupid way to live," thought Marli.

But then a small woman came on, her skin deeply lined, her white clothing edged with a blue border. Something in her face caught Marli's attention. As Mother Teresa bowed her head in prayer, Marli listened and remembered one sentence: "It is by forgetting self that one lives."

Suddenly Marli had a strange feeling. She wished she could have whatever it was Mother Teresa had. Something about her—for some reason she seemed happy inside, even though she lived among the poor in India.

All evening Marli tried to forget Mother Teresa's prayer, but the sentence stayed in her mind. "What does it mean to forget about myself?" Marli wondered.

She tried to push the question away, but the pictures in her memory wouldn't leave. Marli thought of the streets of India, and how she had bugged Mom for a phone of her own. She remembered the hunger and rags, and her desire for another jacket. As much as she wanted to forget the starving bodies she'd seen, she could not.

For the first time in over a year, Marli thought about the choice she'd made when she was nine years old. She had prayed, "Jesus, I want my life to count for

You. I want to tell others about Your love."

Now Marli felt ashamed. She'd avoided God for so long, it felt strange to talk with Him. Yet Marli knew she'd dislike herself even more if she didn't.

"Forgive me, Jesus," she asked, "for always wanting things. Forgive me for always thinking about myself. Show me how I can help others."

As Marli prayed, it felt as though a bag filled with heavy stones fell off her back. Crawling into bed, she slipped between clean sheets and pulled the quilt around her shoulders.

As she nestled down, an idea popped into her head. "Maybe I should offer to babysit Sunny and Jesse. Maybe Mom and Dad would like to go out for breakfast Saturday morning."

As she drifted off to sleep, Marli felt as if she might even like herself again.

TO TALK ABOUT

▶How do you think Marli felt about herself when she kept asking for things? How does selfishness destroy self-esteem?

▶When did Marli's selfish feelings change?

▶What does it mean to deny yourself? Does it mean to hide your good qualities and personality? Or to put away selfish wishes? Which do you think Jesus wants?

▶Marli became an in-spite-of-it kid. How did she start letting God use her right away? How will that kind of growing help her when she gets older?

▶Are there ways in which you've been selfish lately? What are some practical ideas for ways you can help other people?

▶How was Jesus our example in serving others? How will it change your life if you choose to help others?

Jesus said, "If anyone wants to come with me, he must forget himself, take up his cross every day, and follow me. . . . Will a person gain anything if he wins the whole world but is himself lost or defeated? Of course not!" (Luke 9:23, 25, GNB)

I'm sorry, Jesus, for being selfish. Please forgive me. Help me to stop thinking about myself and the things I want. Help me to live the way You did when You were here on earth. I want to serve You.

178

FOR IN-SPITE-OF-IT KIDS

Remember David and how he picked up five stones from the creek? He didn't need more than one for killing Goliath. Yet he had other stones as backup—just in case.

Maybe you've needed only one idea to bring down an enemy of your self-esteem. But you may have picked up several more ideas—just in case. Have you also discovered how often you need to make a choice?

Learning to see yourself as God sees you takes time. Whenever you believe you're worth something to Him, you pick up a stone. You put aside thoughts that would be your enemies. You start forming the habit of letting God love you.

When your self-esteem is based on God's love, you

know you can trust Him. Even though you don't understand why some things happen, you believe Jesus is bigger than your problems. You discover the Holy Spirit helps you with your daily battles. Like David, you become an in-spite-of-it kid.

When you know Jesus and belong to Him, you become all God wants you to be. And your self-esteem comes from Him.

YOU'RE WORTH MORE THAN YOU THINK!